11 CHRISTMAS SONGS FOR SSAA A CAPPELLA

JEFF BRATZ

HarmonyTabs

Sign up for the HarmonyTabs email list to keep up with new
music releases, upcoming publications, and promotions:

HARMONYTABS EMAIL LIST

11 CHRISTMAS SONGS FOR SSAA A CAPPELLA
SECOND EDITION

ISBN: 978-1-961735-10-1 (paperback)
ISBN: 978-1-961735-11-8 (eBook)
ISMN: 979-0-60026-013-3 (paperback)
ISMN: 979-0-60026-014-0 (eBook)

First paperback edition October 2022

Printed in the United States of America

HarmonyTabs Music

HarmonyTabsMusic.com

Contents

Intro

First, thank you for buying this songbook. I know there are a lot of options out there and I'm honored you landed here.

I hope these songs will be as fun for you to sing through as they were for me to arrange. I've always loved the holiday season and I think that's largely due to the music that fills the air in every store, car, home, and everywhere else. I like to believe that in some small part this book will add to the spirit.

On the last page of each song is a QR code. That code will lead you to a homepage for that song where you can find additional resources including audio/video where you can hear the tune and find optional rehearsal tracks.

If at any point you have any questions, comments, suggestions, or anything else, please feel free to drop me a line: Jeff@HarmonyTabs.com.

Happy music-ing!
-Jeff

ANGELS WE HAVE HEARD ON HIGH

AWHHOH (SSAA)
11-11-24

- 1 -

And the moun-tains in re - ply, Ech-o-ing their joy-ous strains.
And the moun-tains in re - ply, Ech-o-ing their joy - ous strains.
What the glad-some ti - dings be which in-spire your heav'n - ly song?
And the moun-tains in re - ply, Ech-o-ing their joy - ous strains.
And the moun-tains in re - ply, Ech-o-ing their joy-ous strains.
Pno.
Glo - - - Glo - - - Glo - - -
Glo - - - - - - - - -
Glo - - - Glo - - - Glo - -
Glo - - - Glo - - - Glo - -
Glo Glo - Glo Glo - Glo Glo -
Pno.

AWHHOH (SSAA)
11-11-24

ANGELS WE HAVE HEARD ON HIGH
20
- RI - A IN EX - CEL - SIS DE - O.
- RI - A IN EX - CEL - SIS DE - O.
- RI - A IN EX - CEL - SIS DE - O.
- RI - A IN EX - CEL - SIS DE - O.
Pno. 
1.
24
IN EX - CEL - SIS DE IN EX - CEL - SIS DE - O.
IN EX - CEL - SIS DE IN EX - CEL - SIS DE - O.
IN EX - CEL - SIS DE IN EX - CEL - SIS DE - O.
IN EX - CEL - SIS DE - IN EX - CEL - SIS DE - O.
2.
Pno.
AWHHOH (SSAA)
11-11-24

Optional Additional Lyrics
(S2 solos on the second verse while the other 3 parts 'Ooh'.
If adding verses, you can choose how you'd like to split this.)

3. Come to Bethlehem and see
Him whose birth the angels sing.
Come, adore on bended knee
Christ the Lord, the newborn King.

4. See within the manger laid
Jesus, Lord of heaven and earth!
Mary, Joseph, lend your aid,
With us sing our Savior's birth.

AWHHOH (SSAA)
11-11-24

AULD LANG SYNE

ALS (SSAA)
11-11-24

- 6 -

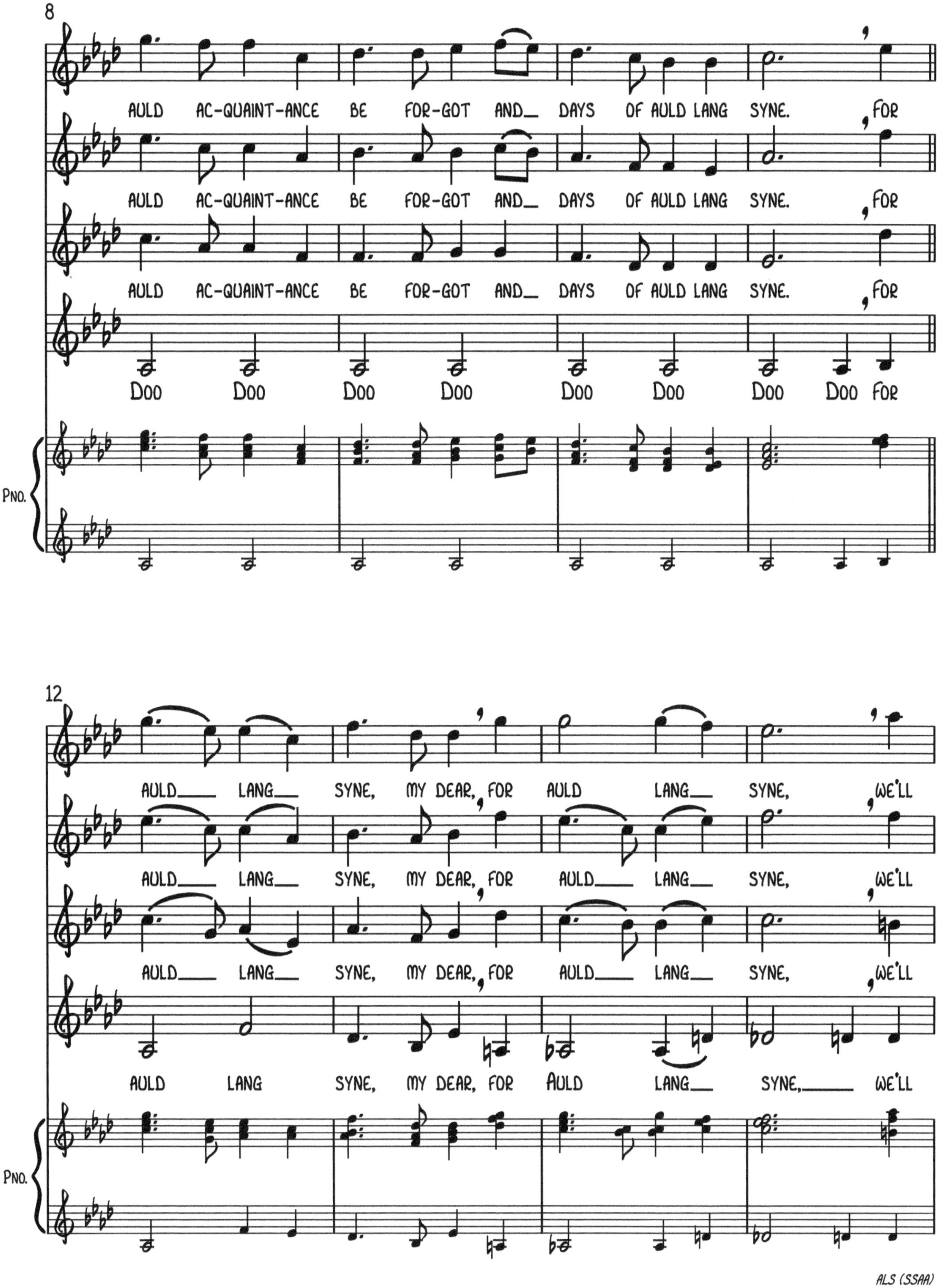
8
AULD AC-QUAINT-ANCE BE FOR-GOT AND_ DAYS OF AULD LANG SYNE. FOR
AULD AC-QUAINT-ANCE BE FOR-GOT AND_ DAYS OF AULD LANG SYNE. FOR
AULD AC-QUAINT-ANCE BE FOR-GOT AND_ DAYS OF AULD LANG SYNE. FOR
DOO DOO DOO DOO DOO DOO DOO DOO FOR
PNO.
12
AULD___ LANG___ SYNE, MY DEAR, FOR AULD LANG___ SYNE, WE'LL
AULD___ LANG___ SYNE, MY DEAR, FOR AULD___ LANG___ SYNE, WE'LL
AULD___ LANG___ SYNE, MY DEAR, FOR AULD___ LANG___ SYNE, WE'LL
AULD LANG SYNE, MY DEAR, FOR AULD LANG___ SYNE,_____ WE'LL
PNO.

16
TAKE A CUP OF KIND - NESS YET FOR AULD LANG SYNE.
TAKE A CUP OF KIND - NESS YET, FOR AULD LANG SYNE.
TAKE A CUP OF KIND - NESS YET, FOR AULD LANG SYNE.
TAKE A CUP OF KIND-NESS YET FOR AULD LANG SYNE.
Pno.

AWAY IN A MANGER

AIAM (SSAA)
11-14-24

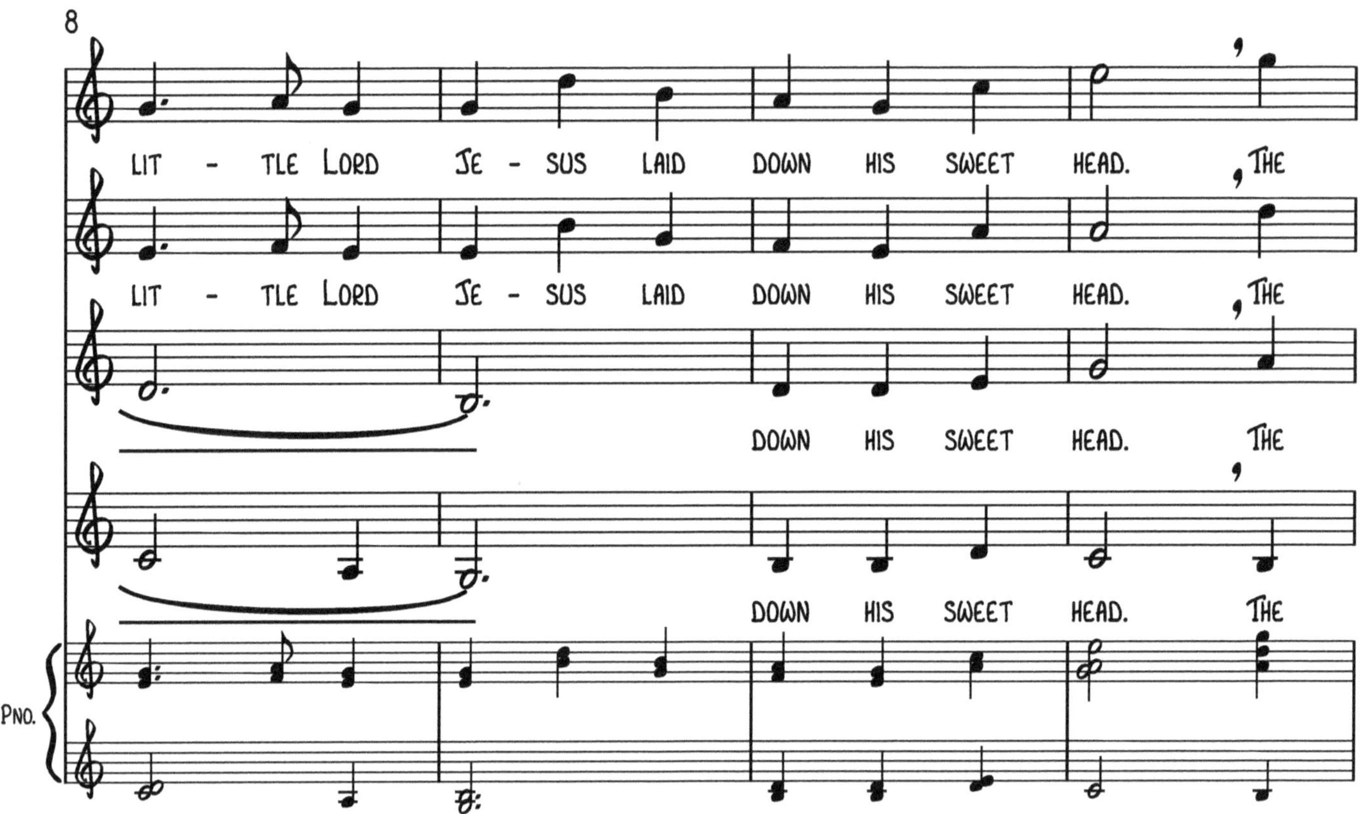
LIT - TLE LORD JE - SUS LAID DOWN HIS SWEET HEAD. , THE
LIT - TLE LORD JE - SUS LAID DOWN HIS SWEET HEAD. , THE
DOWN HIS SWEET HEAD. THE
DOWN HIS SWEET HEAD. THE
PNO.
STARS IN THE SKY____ LOOKED DOWN WHERE HE LAY. THE
STARS IN THE SKY____ LOOKED DOWN WHERE HE LAY.
STARS IN THE SKY____ LOOKED DOWN WHERE HE LAY.
STARS IN THE SKY____ LOOKED DOWN WHERE HE LAY.
PNO.

LIT - TLE LORD JESUS, A - SLEEP ON THE HAY. THE
AH A - SLEEP ON THE HAY. THE
AH A - SLEEP ON THE HAY. THE
AH A - SLEEP ON THE HAY. THE
PNO.
CAT - TLE ARE LOW - ING, THE BA - BY A - WAKES, BUT
CAT - TLE ARE LOW - ING, THE BA - BY A - WAKES, BUT
CAT - TLE ARE LOW - ING, THE BA - BY A - WAKES, BUT
CAT - TLE ARE LOW - ING, THE BA - BY A - WAKES, BUT
PNO.
AIAM (SSAA)
11-14-24

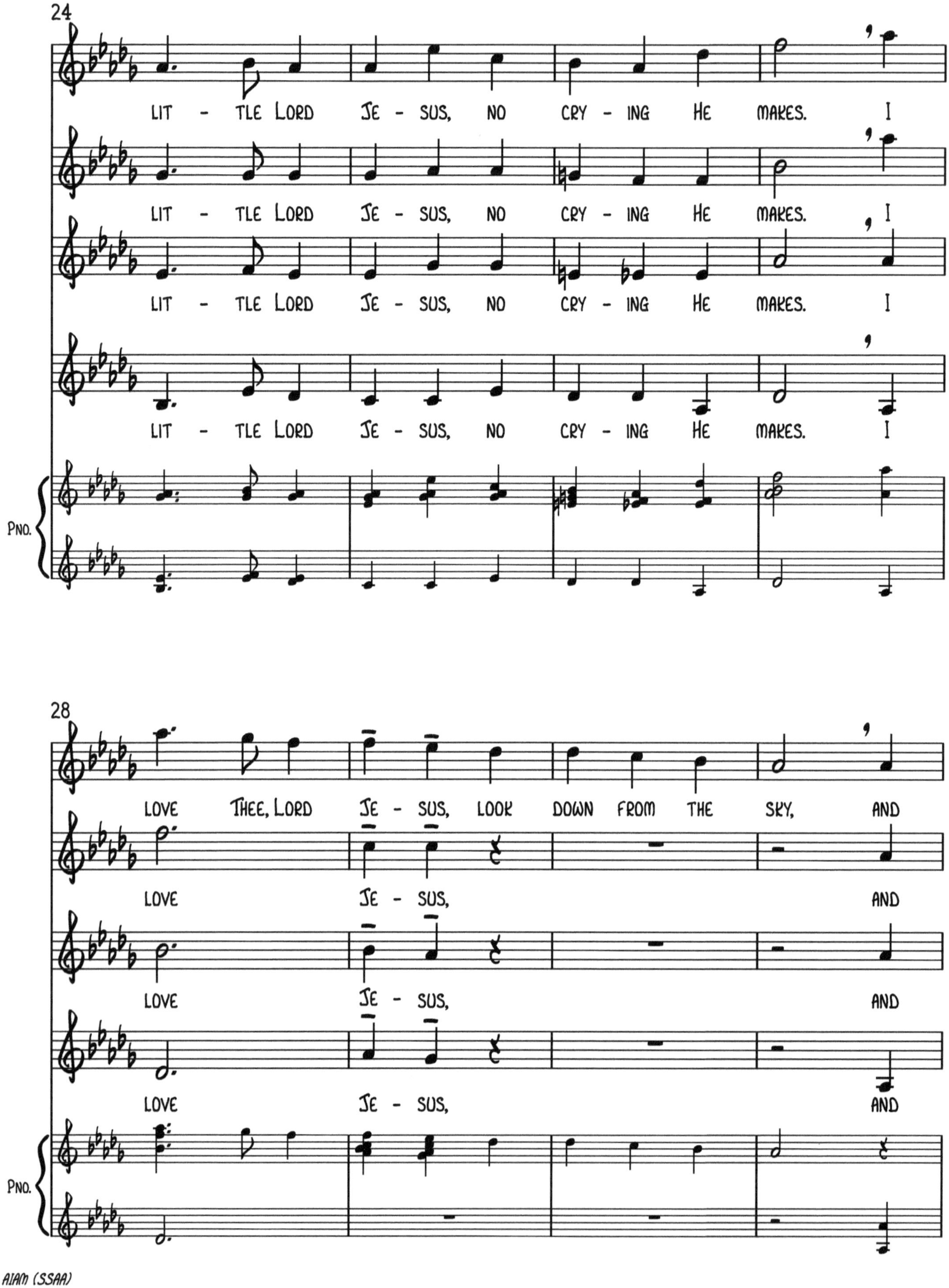

LIT - TLE LORD JE - SUS, NO CRY - ING HE MAKES. I
LIT - TLE LORD JE - SUS, NO CRY - ING HE MAKES. I
LIT - TLE LORD JE - SUS, NO CRY - ING HE MAKES. I
LIT - TLE LORD JE - SUS, NO CRY - ING HE MAKES. I
LOVE THEE, LORD JE - SUS, LOOK DOWN FROM THE SKY, AND
LOVE JE - SUS, AND
LOVE JE - SUS, AND
LOVE JE - SUS, AND

AWAY IN A MANGER

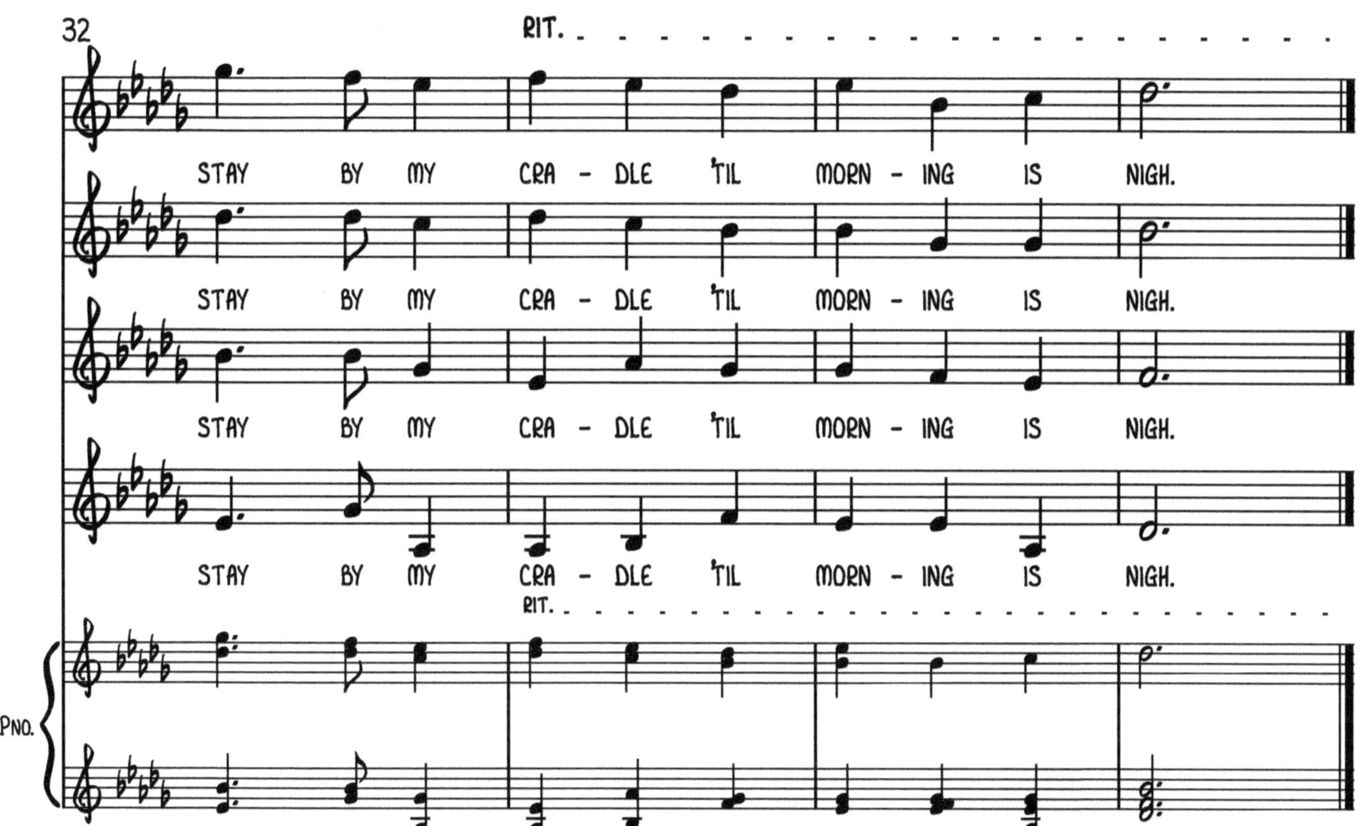

AIAM (SSAA)
11-14-24

DECK THE HALLS

Traditional Welsh Carol
Arr. Jeff Bratz

DECK THE HALLS

DTH (SSAA)
11-18-24

DECK THE HALLS

15

THE AN - CIENT YULE-TIDE CAR - OL, FA, LA, LA, LA, LA, LA, LA, LA, LA.

THE AN - CIENT YULE-TIDE CAR - OL, FA, LA, LA, LA, LA, LA, LA, LA, LA.

THE AN - CIENT YULE-TIDE CAR - OL, FA, LA, LA, LA, LA, LA, LA, LA, LA.

THE AN - CIENT YULE-TIDE CAR - OL, FA, LA, LA, LA, LA, LA, LA, LA, LA.

Pno.

19

STRAIGHT

SWING

MAKE ALL FOLLOWING 'STRAIGHT' SECTIONS A MORE CLASSICAL SOUND, BUT KEEP THE JAZZ SOUND FOR THE 'SWING' SECTIONS

SEE THE BLAZ-ING YULE BE-FORE US, FA, LA, LA, LA, LA, LA, LA, LA, LA.

SEE THE BLAZ-ING YULE BE-FORE US, FA, LA, LA, LA, LA, LA, LA, LA, LA.

SEE THE BLAZ-ING YULE BE-FORE US, FA, LA, LA, LA, LA, LA, LA, LA, LA.

SEE THE BLAZ-ING YULE BE-FORE US, FA, LA, LA, LA, LA, LA, LA, LA, LA.

STRAIGHT

SWING

Pno.

DTH (SSAA)
11-18-24

DECK THE HALLS

31
STRAIGHT
SWING
WHILE I TELL OF YULE-TIDE TREAS-URE, FA, LA, LA, LA, LA, LA, LA, LA, LA.
WHILE I TELL OF YULE-TIDE TREAS-URE, FA, LA, LA, LA, LA, LA, LA, LA, LA.
WHILE I TELL OF YULE-TIDE TREAS-URE, FA, LA, LA, LA, LA, LA, LA, LA, LA.
WHILE I TELL OF YULE-TIDE TREAS-URE, FA, LA, LA, LA, LA, LA, LA, LA, LA.
STRAIGHT
SWING
PNO.
♩=210 (SWING)
♩=150 STRAIGHT
35
mp - HUSHED, LIKE A SECRET
mf - UN-HUSHED
FAST A-WAY THE OLD YEAR_ PASS - ES, FA, LA, LA, LA, LA, LA, LA, LA, LA.
FAST A-WAY THE OLD YEAR_ PASS - ES, FA, LA, LA, LA, LA, LA, LA, LA, LA.
FAST A-WAY THE OLD YEAR_ PASS - ES, FA, LA, LA, LA, LA, LA, LA, LA, LA.
FAST A-WAY THE OLD YEAR_ PASS - ES, FA, LA, LA, LA, LA, LA, LA, LA, LA.
♩=210 (SWING)
♩=150 STRAIGHT
PNO.

DECK THE HALLS

DTH (SSAA)
11-18-24

DECK THE HALLS

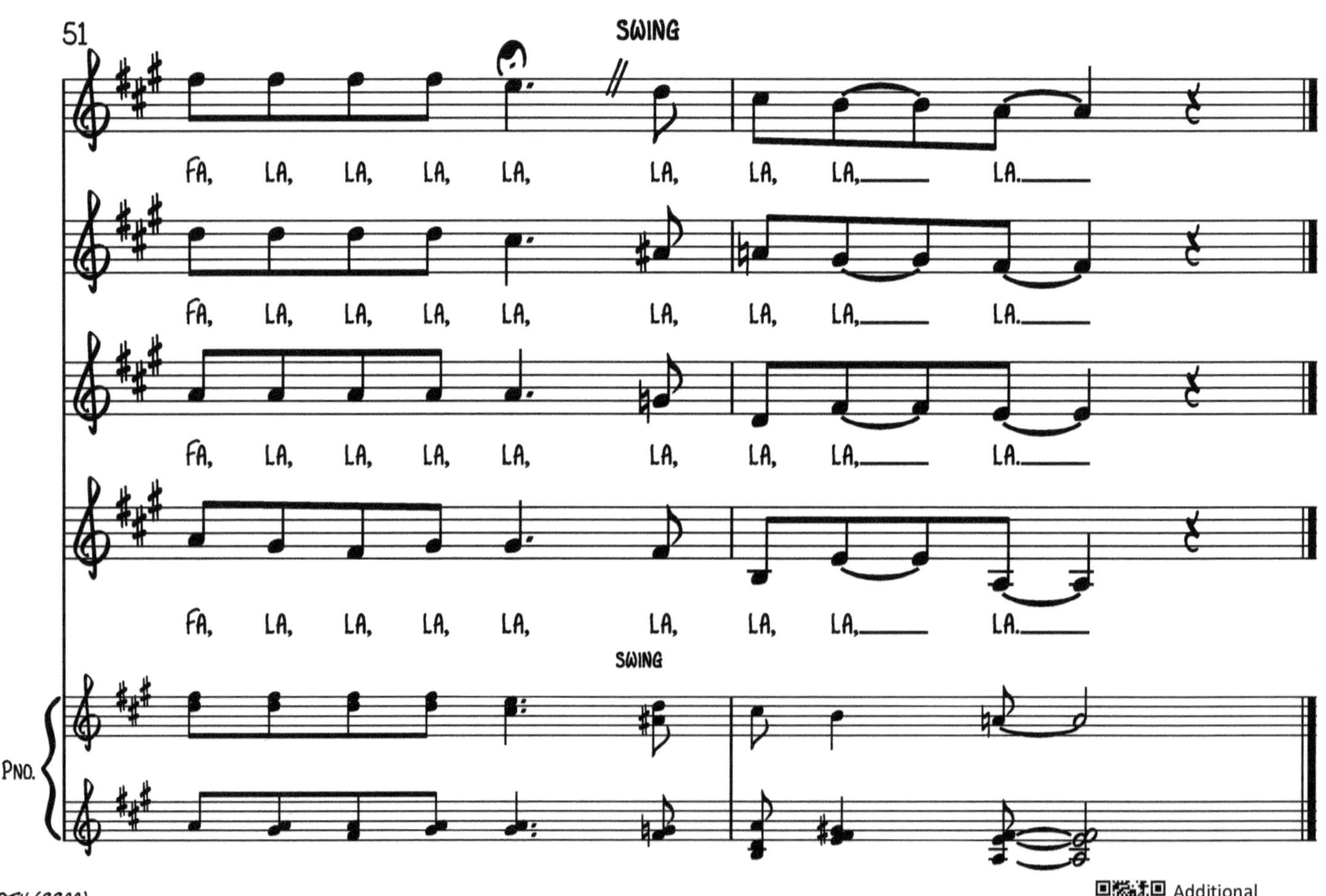

DTH (SSAA)
11-18-24

THE FIRST NOEL

TFN (SSAA)
11-19-24

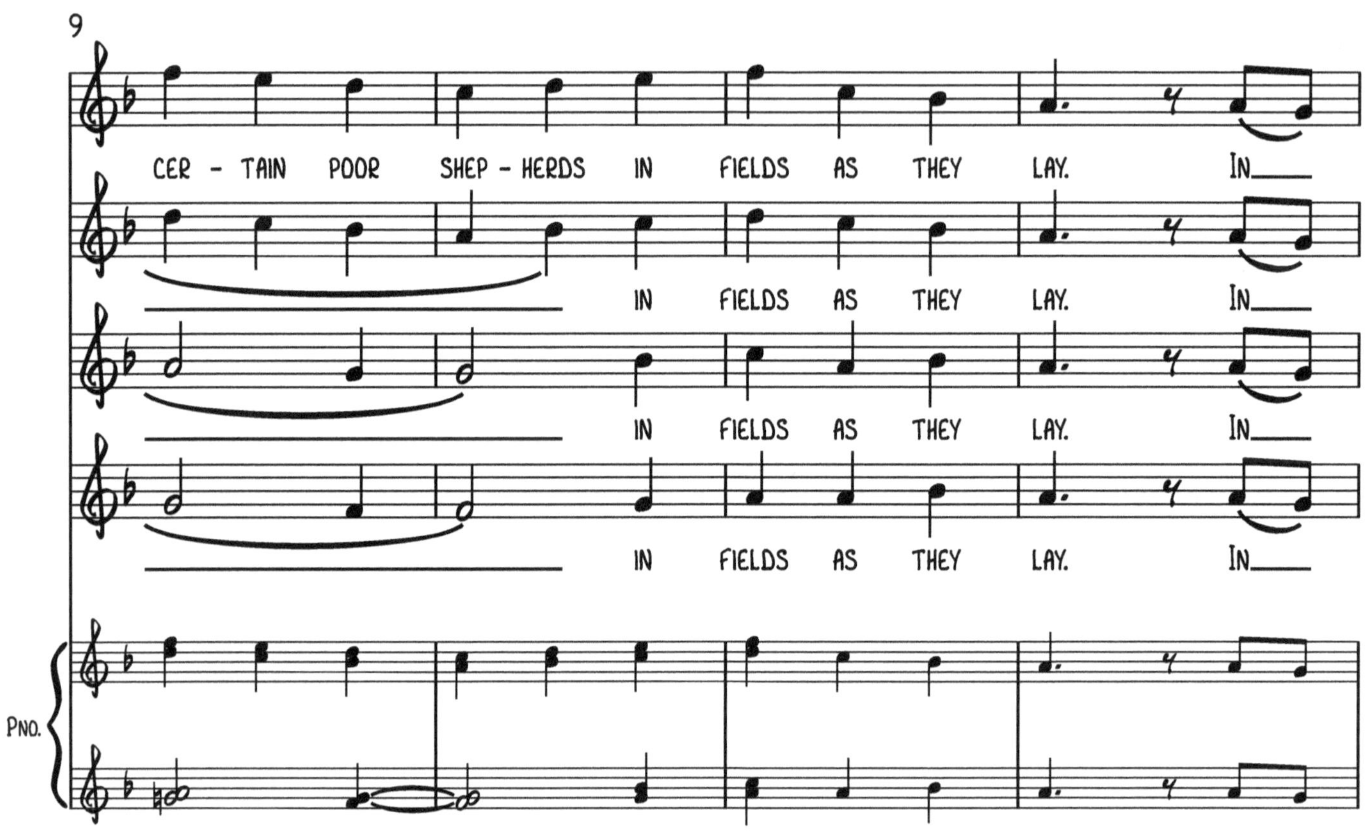

9
CER - TAIN POOR SHEP - HERDS IN FIELDS AS THEY LAY. IN
IN FIELDS AS THEY LAY. IN
IN FIELDS AS THEY LAY. IN
IN FIELDS AS THEY LAY. IN
PNO.

13
FIELDS WHERE THEY LAY KEEP - ING THEIR SHEEP, ON A
FIELDS WHERE THEY LAY KEEP - ING THEIR SHEEP, ON A
FIELDS WHERE THEY LAY KEEP - ING THEIR SHEEP, ON A
FIELDS WHERE THEY LAY KEEP - ING THEIR SHEEP, ON A
PNO.

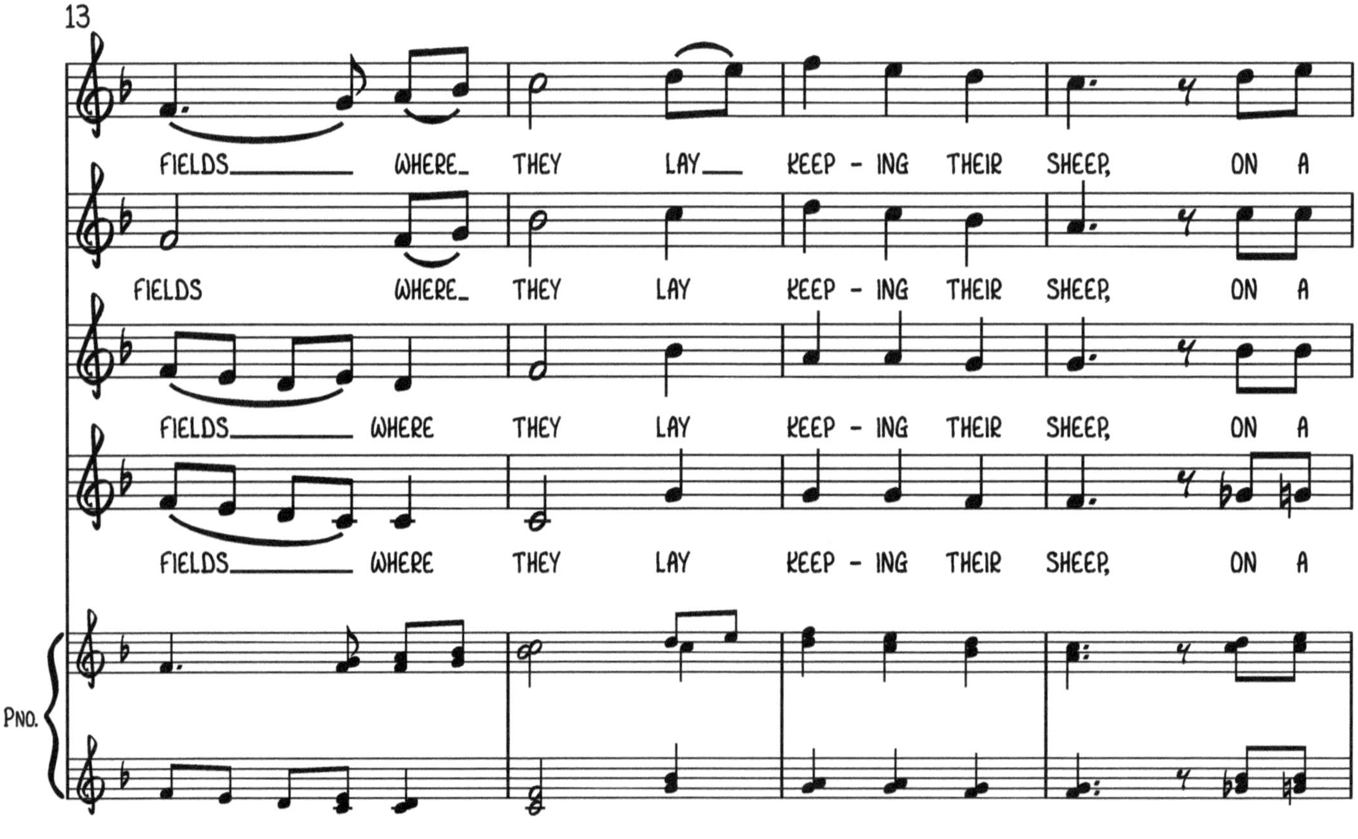

17
COLD WIN - TER'S NIGHT THAT WAS SO DEEP. NO -
N.B.
COLD NIGHT THAT WAS SO DEEP. NO -
N.B.
COLD NIGHT THAT WAS SO DEEP. NO -
N.B.
COLD NIGHT THAT WAS SO DEEP. NO -
PNO.

21
- EL, NO - EL, NO - EL, NO - EL,
- EL, NO - EL, NO - EL, NO - EL,
EL, NO - EL, NO - EL, NO - EL,
- EL, NO - EL, NO - EL, NO - EL,
PNO.

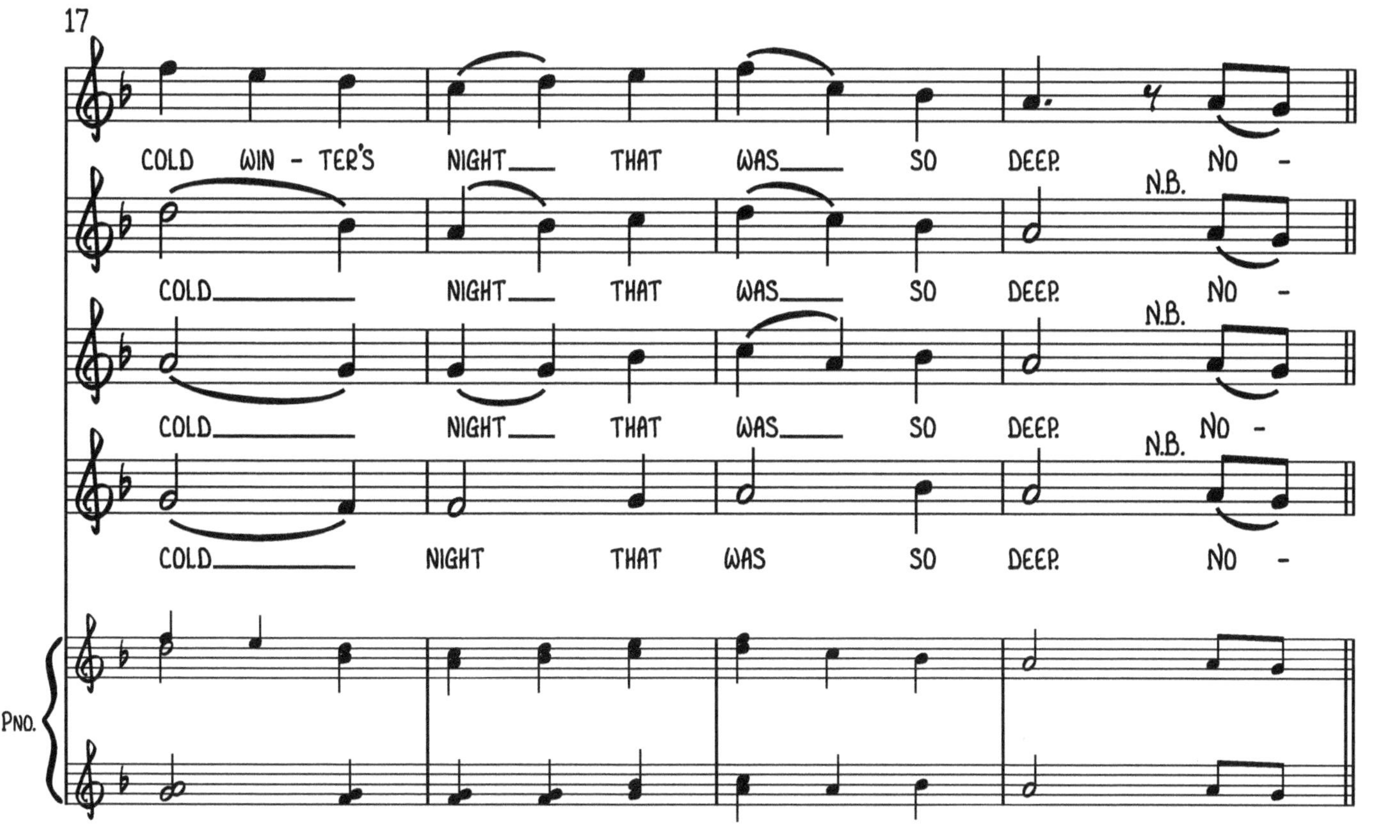

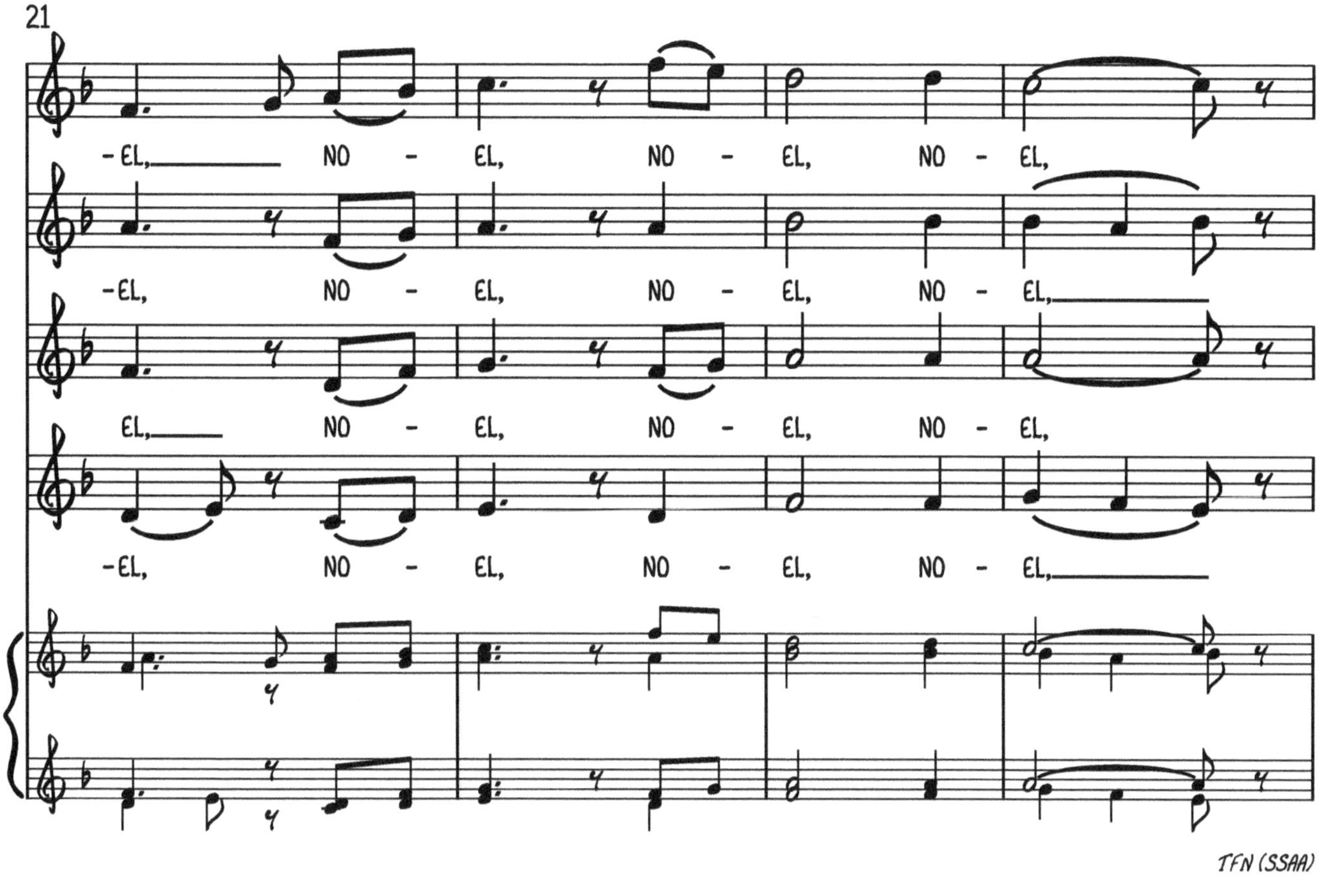

THE FIRST NOEL
25
BORN IS THE KING OF IS - RA - EL. NO -
BORN IS THE KING OF IS - RA - EL. NO -
BORN IS THE KING OF IS - RA - EL. NO -
BORN IS THE KING OF IS - RA - EL. NO -
Pno.
29 
-EL, NO - EL, NO - EL, NO - EL,
-EL, NO - EL, NO - EL, NO - EL,
-EL, NO - EL, NO - EL, NO - EL,
-EL, NO - EL, NO - EL, NO - EL,
Pno.
TFN (SSAA)
11-19-24

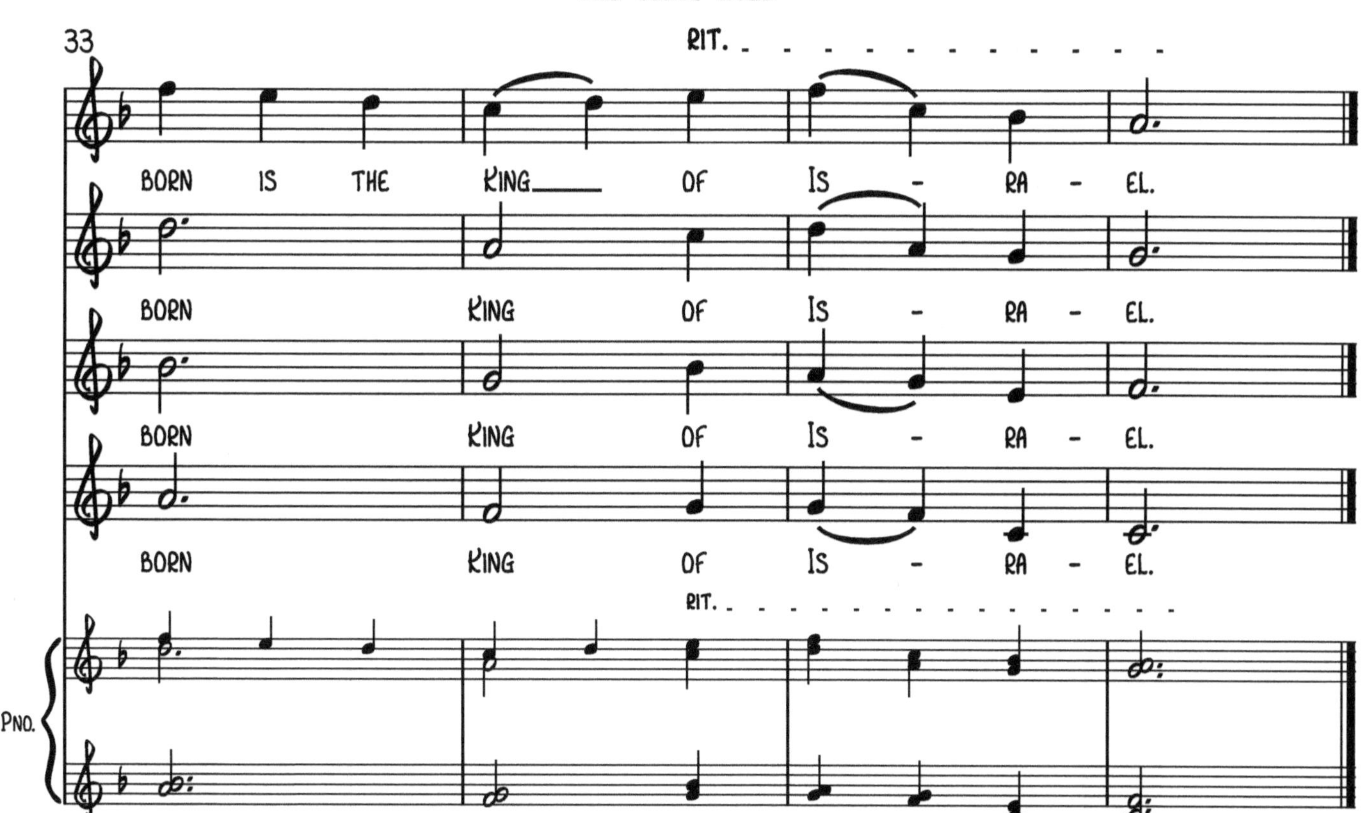

TFN (SSAA)
11-19-24

GO TELL IT ON THE MOUNTAIN

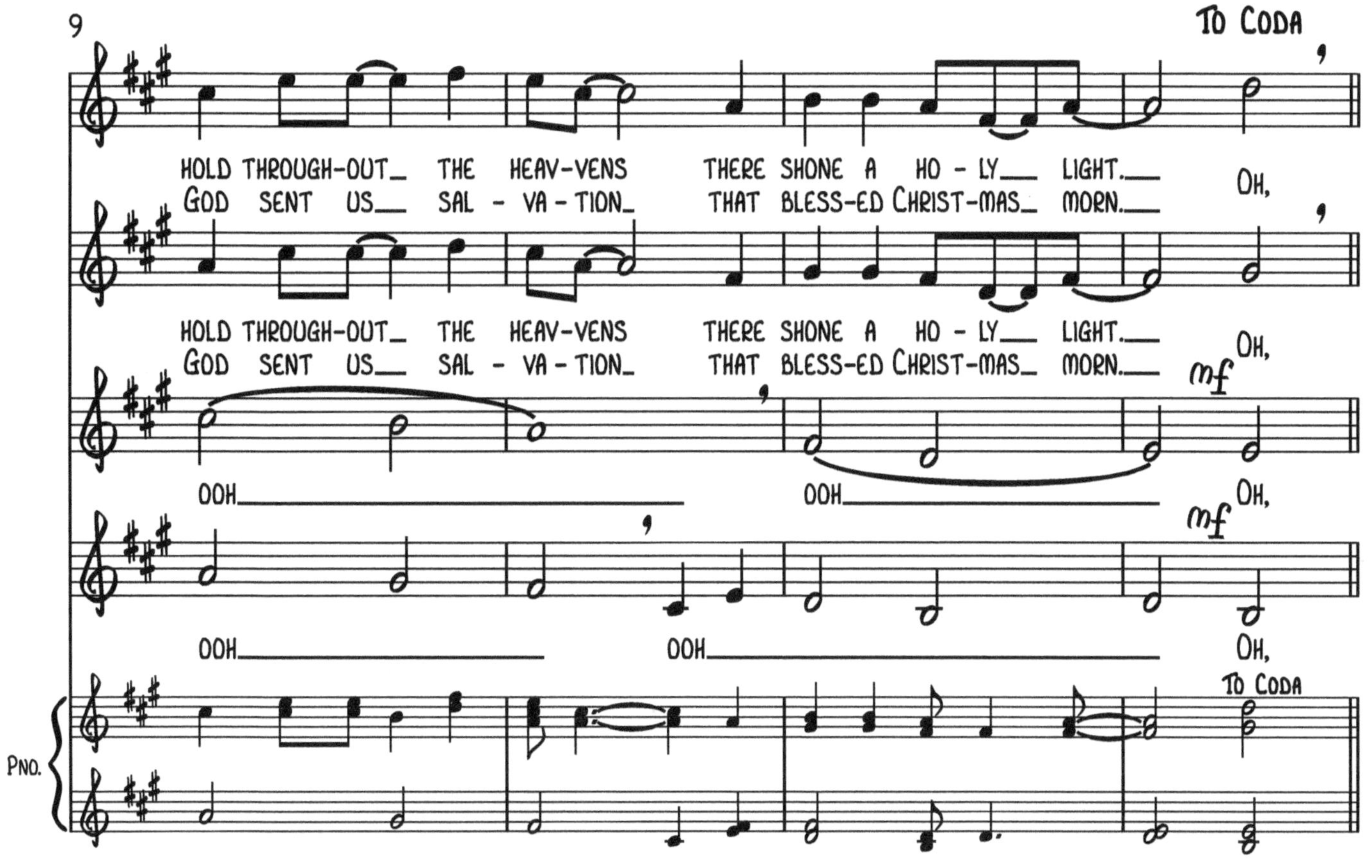

GO TELL IT ON THE MOUNTAIN
9
TO CODA
HOLD THROUGH-OUT_ THE HEAV-VENS THERE SHONE A HO - LY___ LIGHT.___ Oh,
GOD SENT US__ SAL - VA-TION_ THAT BLESS-ED CHRIST-MAS_ MORN.___ Oh,
HOLD THROUGH-OUT_ THE HEAV-VENS THERE SHONE A HO - LY___ LIGHT.___ Oh,
GOD SENT US__ SAL - VA-TION_ THAT BLESS-ED CHRIST-MAS_ MORN.___ Oh,
OOH_ OOH_ Oh,
OOH_ OOH_ Oh,
mf
mf
Pno.
TO CODA
13
GO TELL IT ON THE MOUN - TAIN O - VER THE HILLS AND EV - R'Y - WHERE._
GO TELL IT ON THE MOUN - TAIN O - VER THE HILLS AND EV - R'Y - WHERE._
GO TELL IT ON THE MOUN - TAIN O - VER THE HILLS AND EV - R'Y-WHERE.
GO TELL IT ON THE MOUN - TAIN O - VER THE HILLS AND EV - R'Y-WHERE.
Pno.
GT IOTm (SSAA)
11-21-24

GO TELL IT ON THE MOUNTAIN
17
D.S. AL CODA
Go tell it on the moun - tain that Je - sus Christ is born. Down
Go tell it on the moun - tain that Je - sus Christ is born. Down
Go tell it on the moun - tain that Je - sus Christ is born.
Go tell it on the moun - tain that Je - sus Christ is born.
Go tell it on the moun - tain that Je - sus Christ is born. D.S. al Coda
Pno.
21 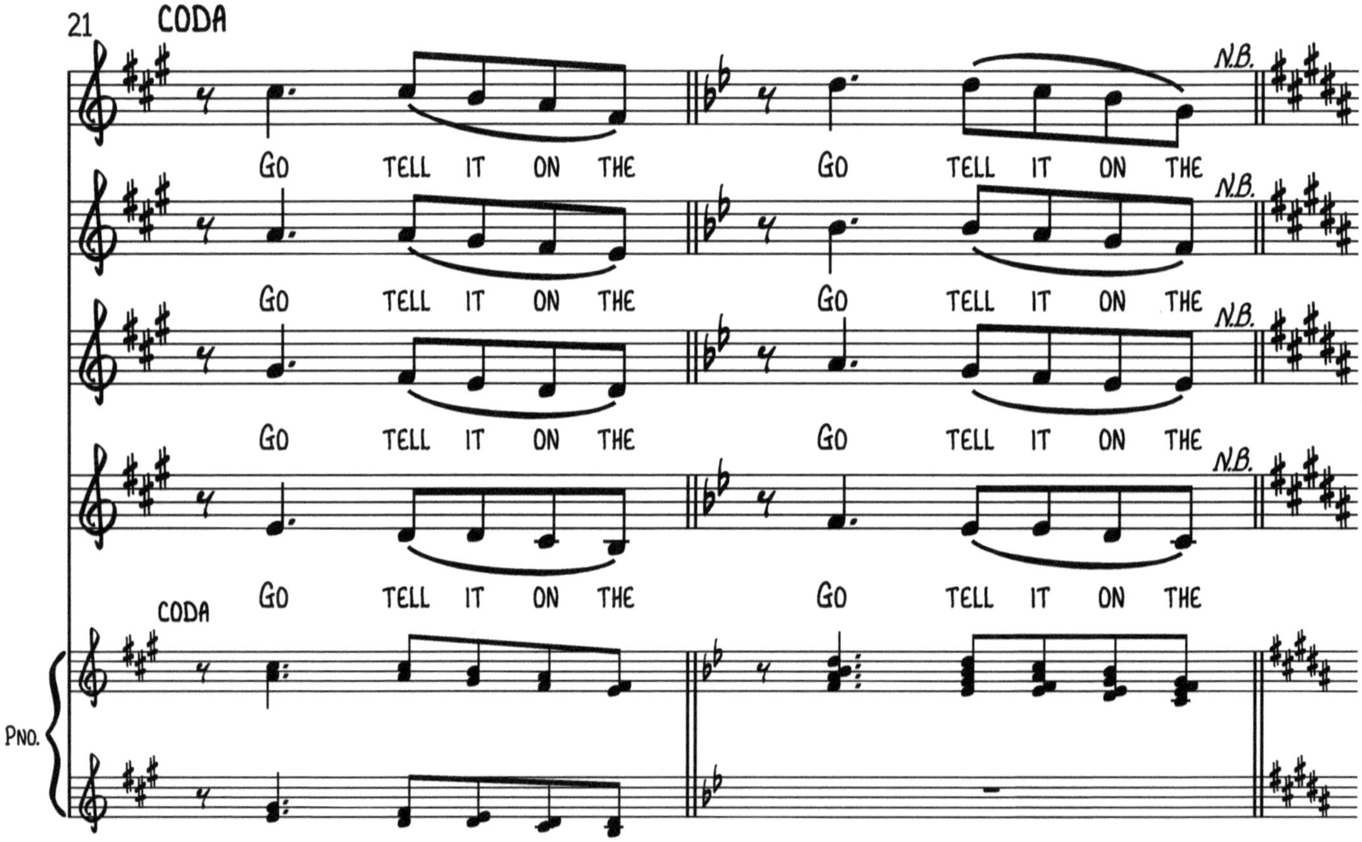
CODA
N.B.
Go tell it on the Go tell it on the
Go tell it on the Go tell it on the
Go tell it on the Go tell it on the
Go tell it on the Go tell it on the
CODA Go tell it on the Go tell it on the
Pno.
GT IOT'm (SSAA)
11-21-24

Go tell it on the moun - tain , o - ver the hills and ev - r'y - where.
Go tell it on the moun - tain , o - ver the hills and ev - r'y - where.
Go tell it on the moun - tain , o - ver the hills and ev - r'y-where.
Go tell it on the moun - tain o - ver the hills and ev - r'y-where.
Pno.

Go tell it on the moun - tain that Je - sus Christ is born. , That
Go tell it on the moun - tain that Je - sus Christ is born. , That
Go tell it on the moun - tain that Je - sus Christ is born. , That
Go tell it on the moun - tain that Je - sus Christ is born. , That
Go tell it on the moun - tain that Je - sus Christ is born. That
Pno.

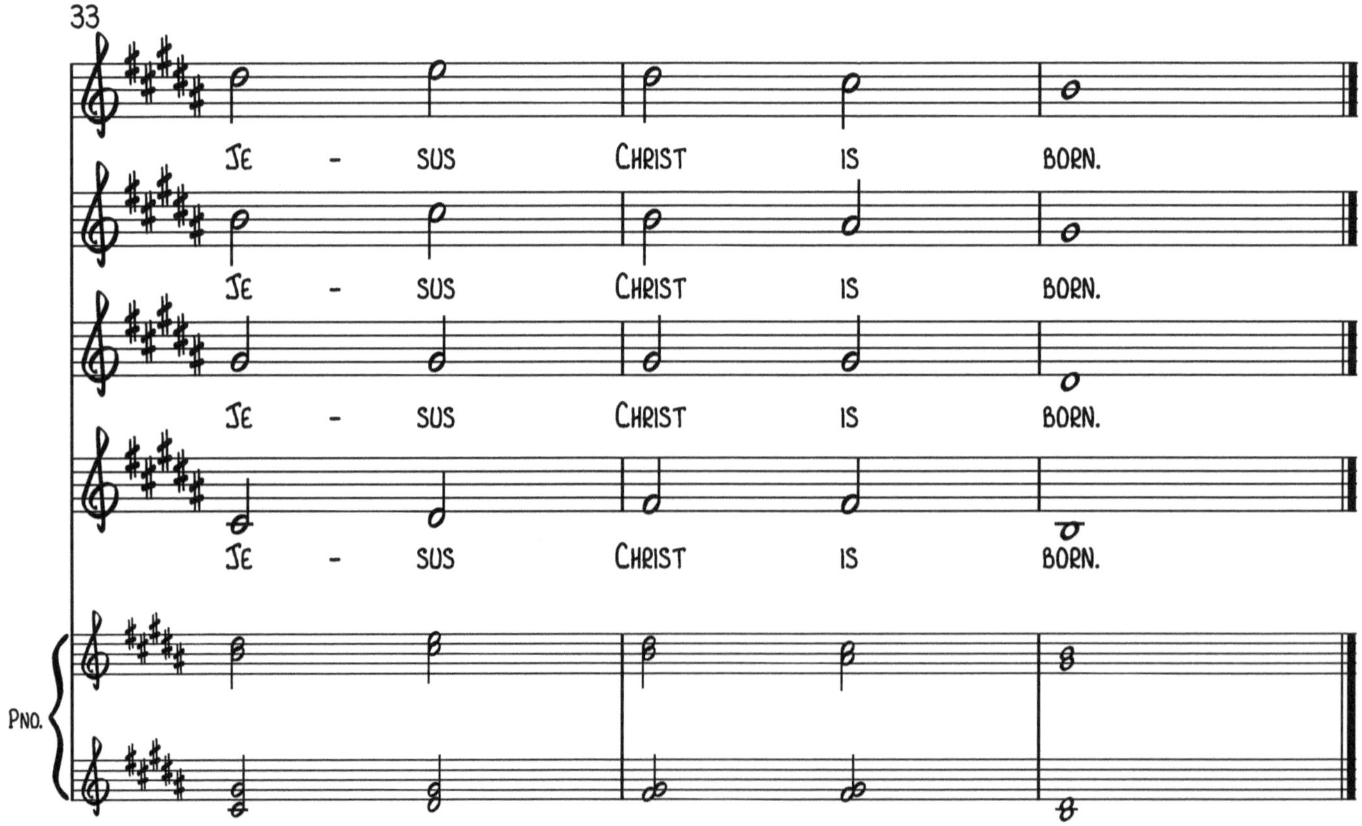

GT1OTm (SSAA)
11-21-24

Additional resources for this arrangement

GOD REST YE MERRY, GENTLEMEN

GRYMG (SSAA)
11-22-24

SAVE US ALL FROM SA-TAN'S POW'R WHEN WE WERE GONE A-STRAY. OH,
SAVE US ALL FROM SA-TAN'S POW'R WHEN WE WERE GONE A-STRAY. OH,
DOO DOO
DOO DOO
Pno.

TI - DINGS OF COM - FORT AND JOY, COM-FORT AND JOY. OH,
TI - DINGS OF COM - FORT AND JOY, COM-FORT AND JOY. OH,
DOO DOO
DOO DOO
Pno.

GOD REST YE MERRY, GENTLEMEN
18
TI - DINGS OF COM - FORT AND JOY. JOY. FROM
TI - DINGS OF COM - FORT AND JOY. JOY.
DOO DOO
DOO DOO
Pno.
22
mp
f
GOD OUR HEAV'N - LY FA - THER A BLESS - ED AN - GEL CAME, AND
f mp
FROM GOD OUR HEAV'N - LY FA - THER A
f mp
FROM GOD OUR HEAV'N - LY FA - THER A BLESS - ED AN - GEL
f
FROM GOD OUR HEAV'N - LY
Pno.
GRY MG (SSAA)
11-22-24

GOD REST YE MERRY, GENTLEMEN

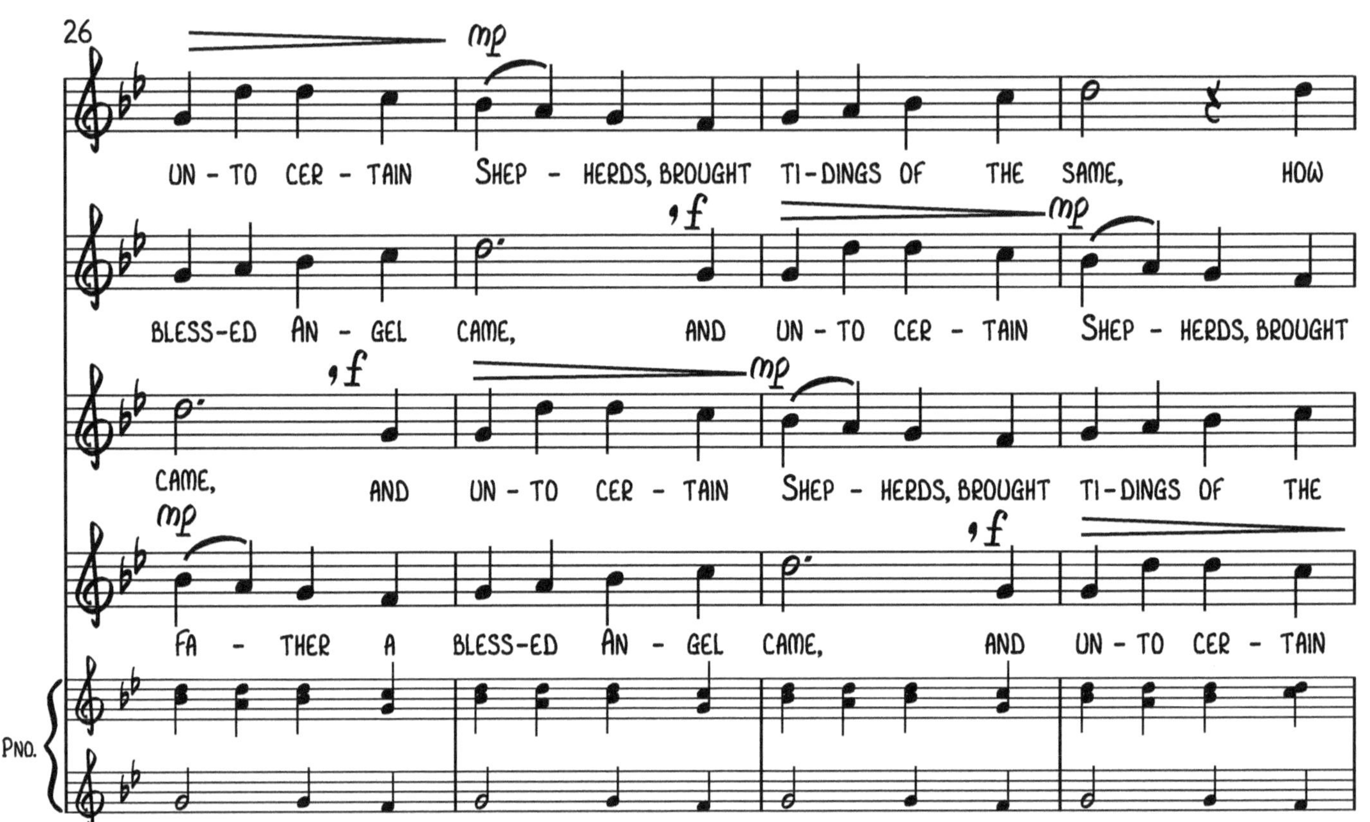

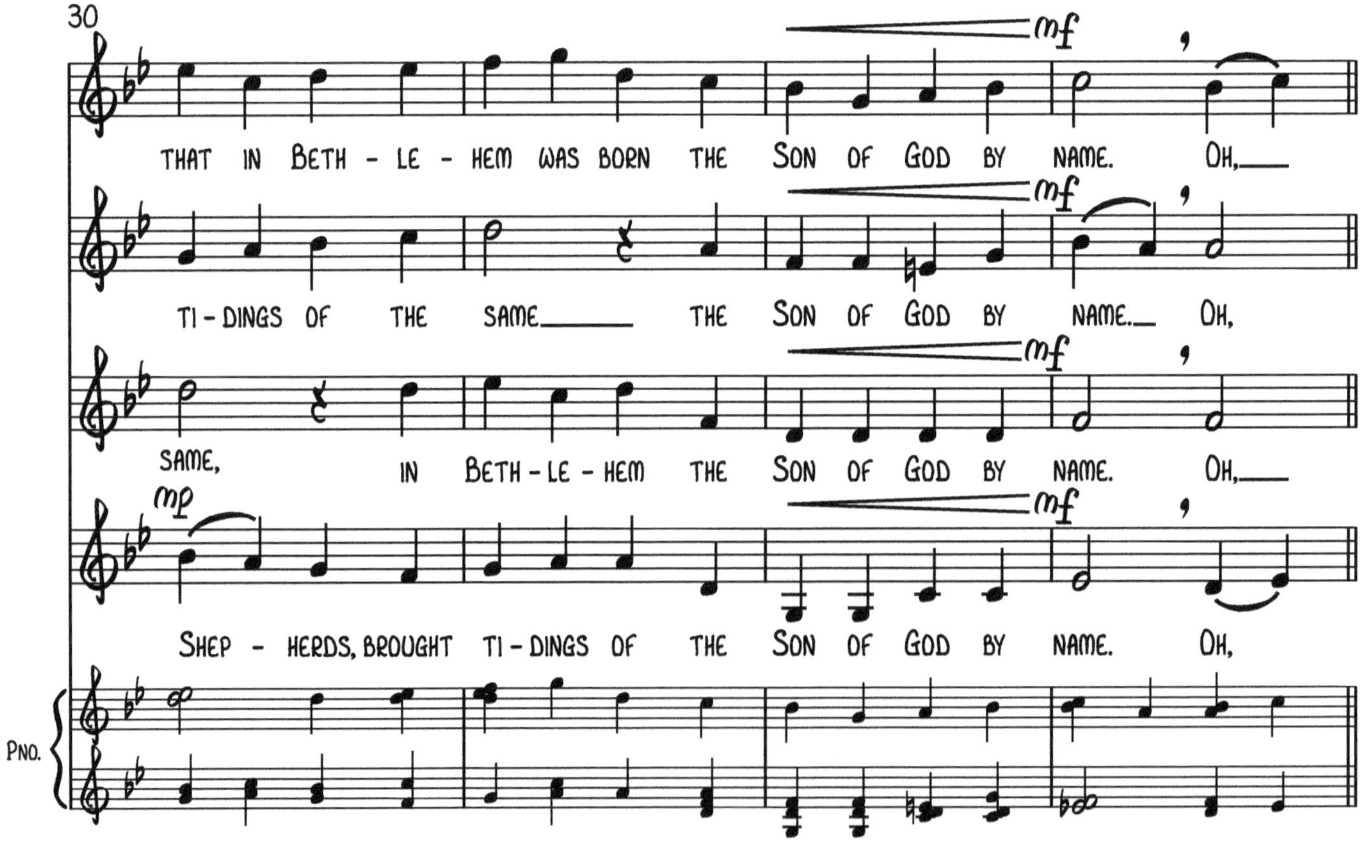

GRY MG (SSAA)
11-22-24

34
TI - DINGS OF COM - FORT AND JOY, COM-FORT AND JOY. Oh,___
TI - DINGS OF COM - FORT AND JOY, COM-FORT AND JOY.___ , Oh,___
TI - DINGS OF COM - FORT AND JOY, COM-FORT AND JOY. , Oh,
TI - DINGS OF COM - FORT AND JOY, COM-FORT AND JOY. Oh,___
Pno.

38
TI - DINGS OF COM - FORT , TI - DINGS OF COM - FORT
TI - DINGS OF COM - FORT , TI - DINGS OF COM - FORT
TI - DINGS OF COM - FORT , TI - DINGS OF COM - FORT
TI - DINGS OF COM - FORT TI - DINGS OF COM - FORT
Pno.

GRY MG (SSAA)
11-22-24

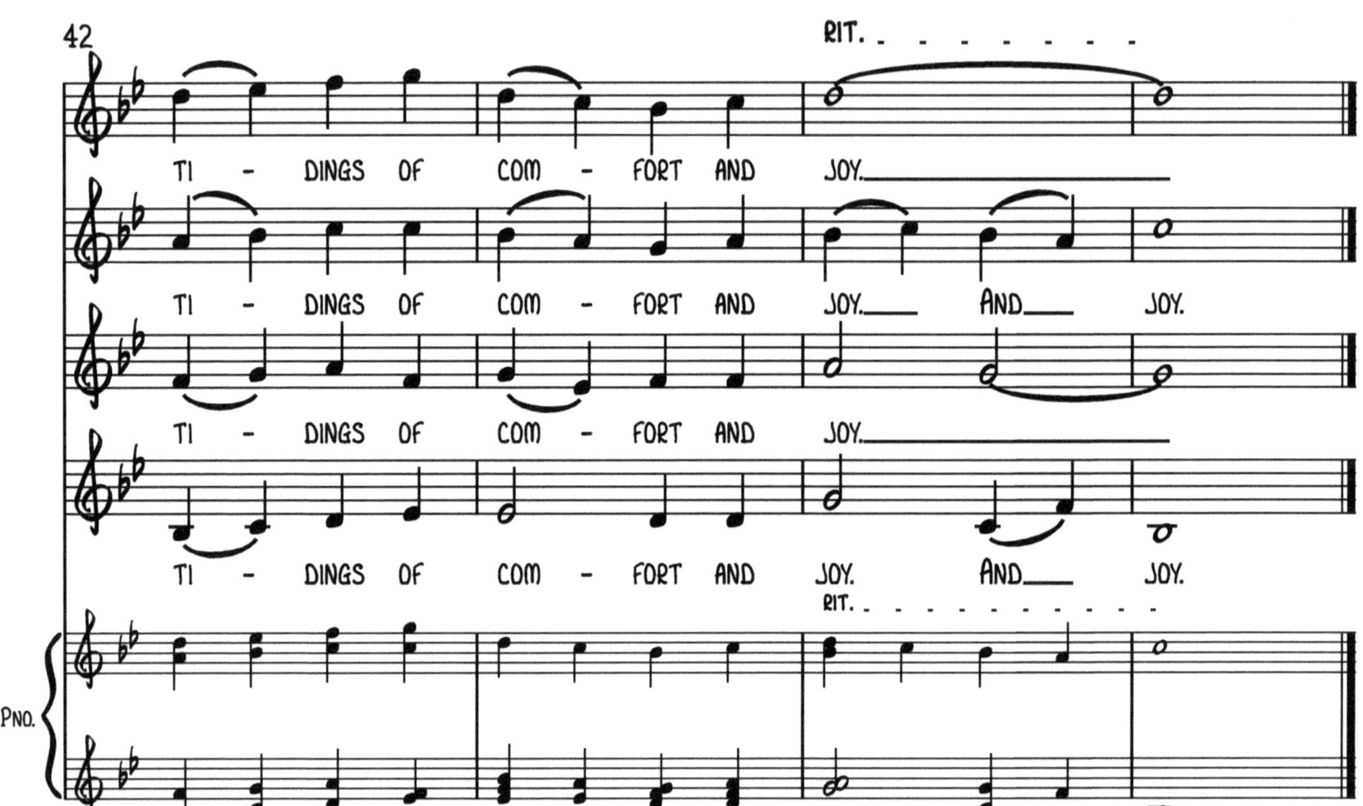

GRY/MG (SSAA)
11-22-24

HALLELUJAH CHORUS
(ABRIDGED)

George Friedrich Handel
arr. Jeff Bratz

HC (SSAA)
11-26-24

7
LU - JAH! HAL - LE - LU - JAH! HAL - LE - LU - JAH!
LU - JAH! HAL - LE - LU - JAH! HAL - LE - LU - JAH!
LU - JAH! HAL - LE - LU - JAH! HAL - LE - LU - JAH!
LU - JAH! HAL - LE - LU - JAH! HAL - LE - LU - JAH!
PNO.

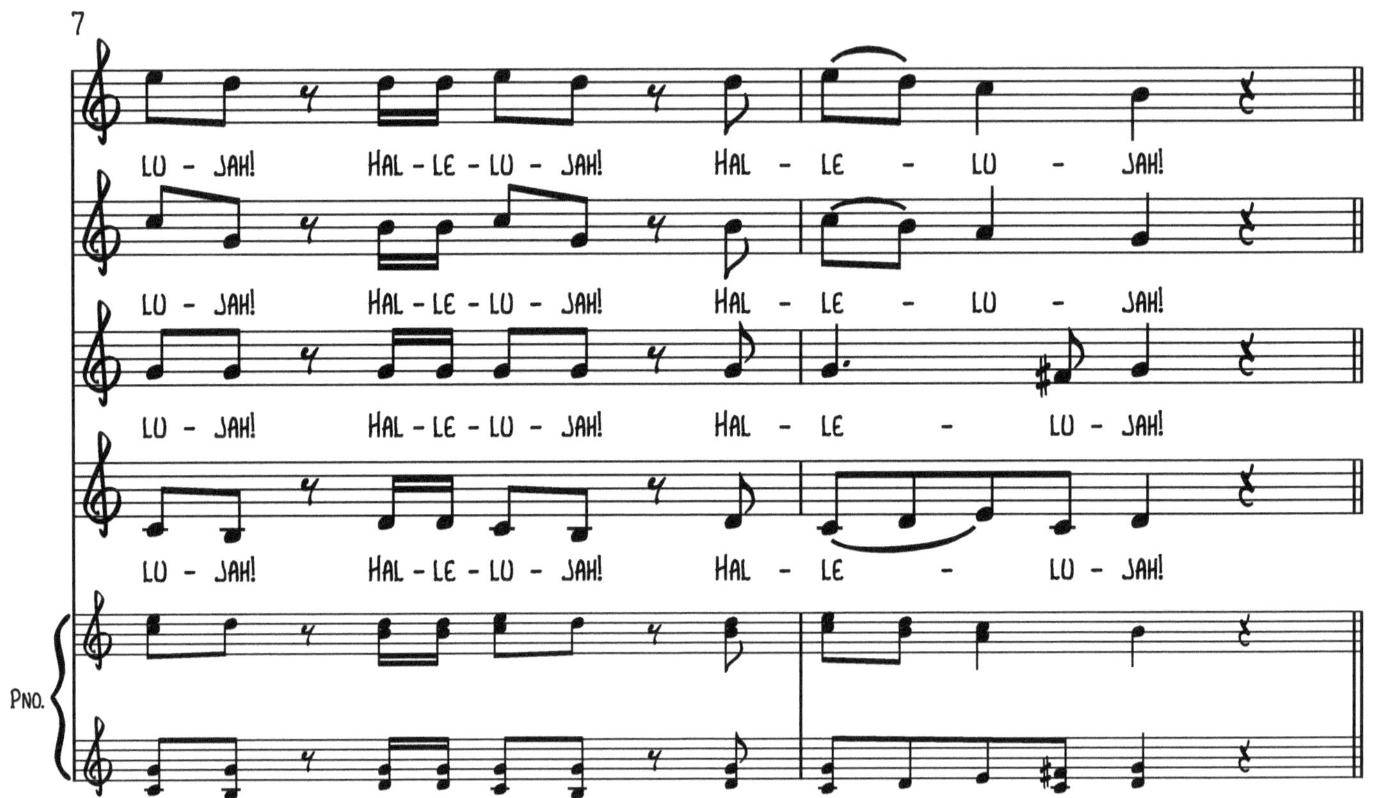

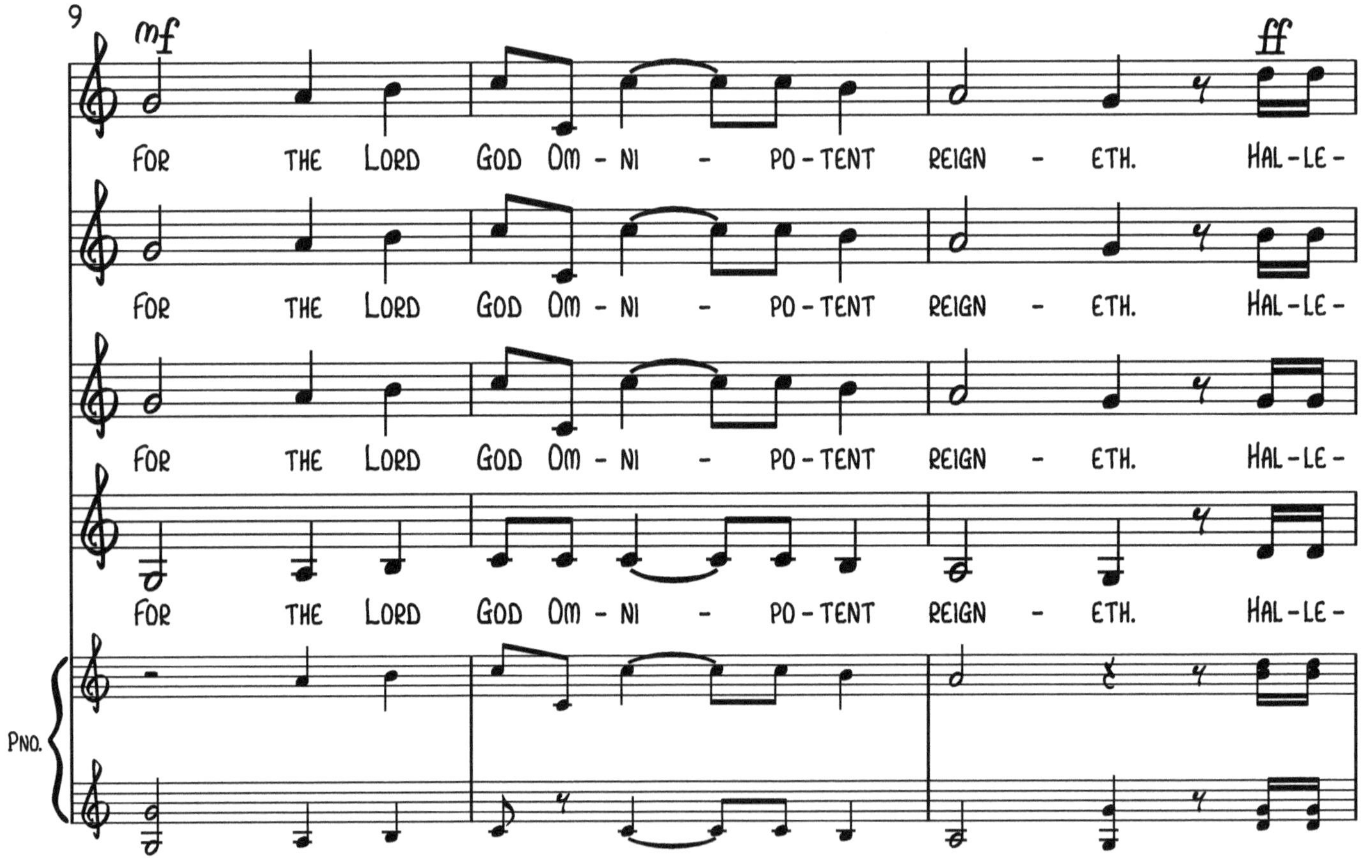
9
mf
ff
FOR THE LORD GOD OM - NI - PO - TENT REIGN - ETH. HAL - LE -
FOR THE LORD GOD OM - NI - PO - TENT REIGN - ETH. HAL - LE -
FOR THE LORD GOD OM - NI - PO - TENT REIGN - ETH. HAL - LE -
FOR THE LORD GOD OM - NI - PO - TENT REIGN - ETH. HAL - LE -
PNO.

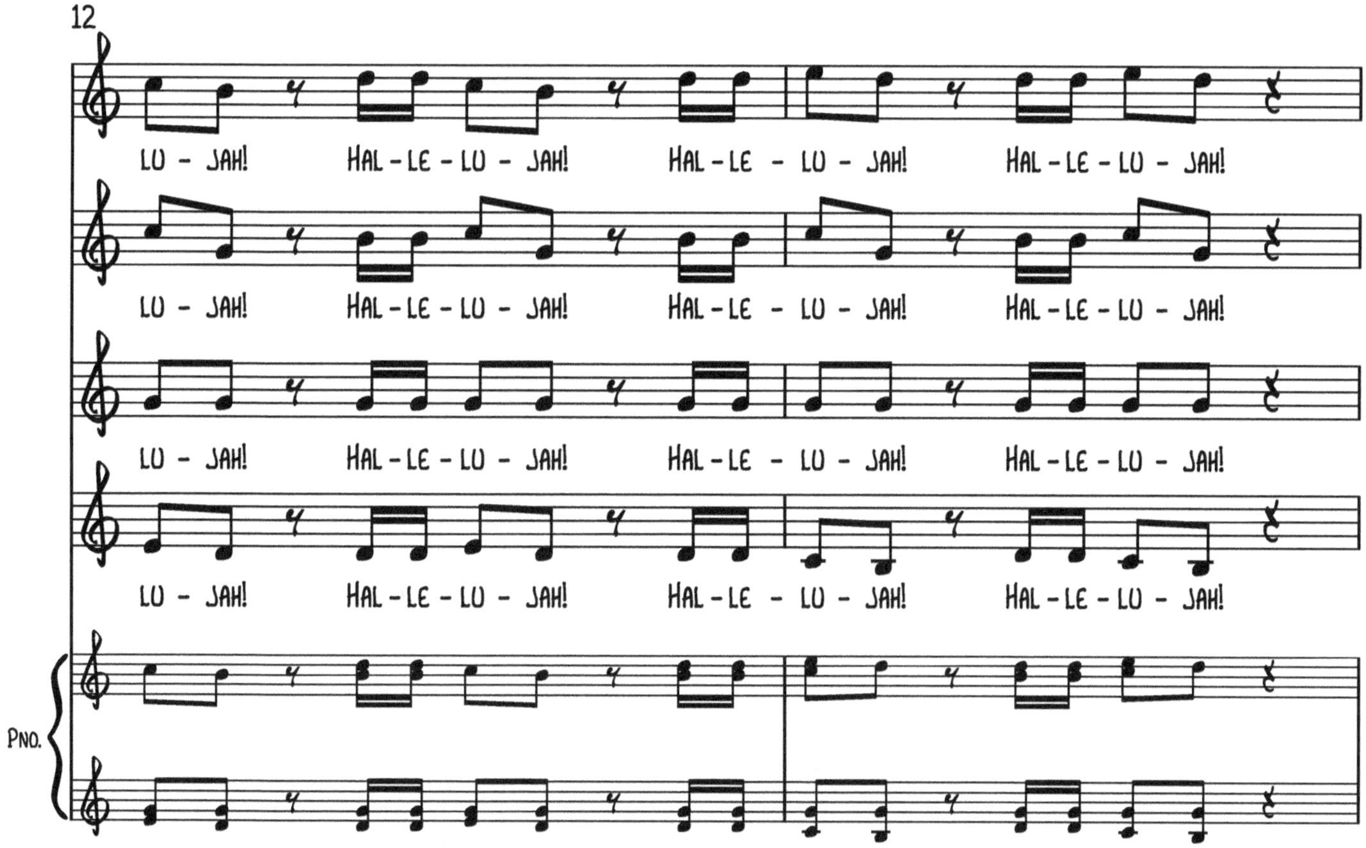

HALLELUJAH CHORUS (ABRIDGED)

HC (SSAA)
11-26-24

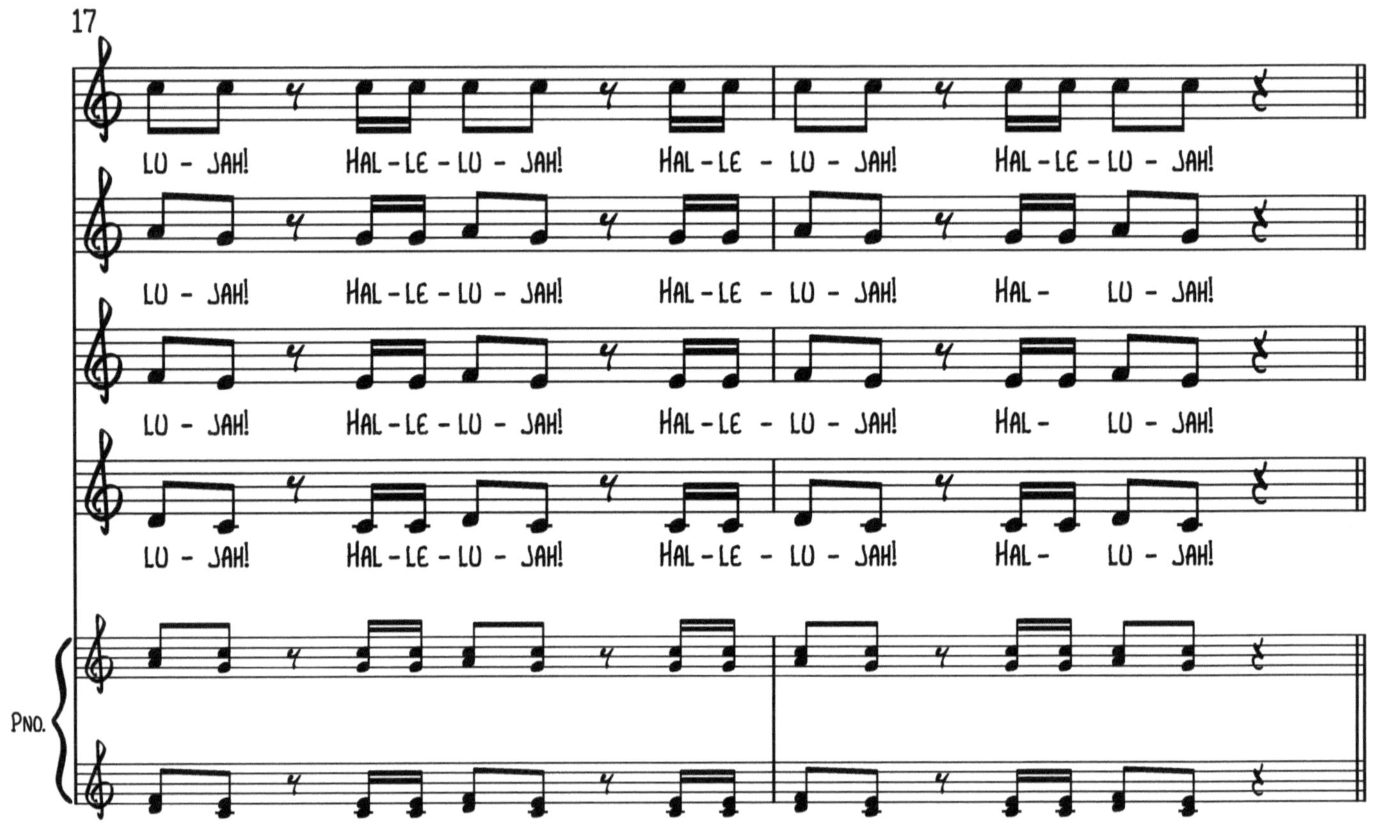
17
LU – JAH! HAL – LE – LU – JAH! HAL – LE – LU – JAH! HAL – LE – LU – JAH!
LU – JAH! HAL – LE – LU – JAH! HAL – LE – LU – JAH! HAL – LU – JAH!
LU – JAH! HAL – LE – LU – JAH! HAL – LE – LU – JAH! HAL – LU – JAH!
LU – JAH! HAL – LE – LU – JAH! HAL – LE – LU – JAH! HAL – LU – JAH!
PNO.

19
f
mf
AND HE SHALL REIGN FOR – EV – ER AND EV – ER, FOR EV – ER AND
f
AND HE SHALL REIGN FOR
PNO.

HALLELUJAH CHORUS (ABRIDGED)

30
KINGS, AND LORD OF
KINGS, AND LORD OF
ff
FOR EV-ER AND EV-ER. HAL-LE-LU-JAH! HAL-LE-LU-JAH!
FOR EV-ER AND EV-ER. HAL-LE-LU-JAH! HAL-LE-LU-JAH!
PNO.
33
LORDS. HAL-LE-LU-JAH! HAL-LE-LU-JAH! HAL-
LORDS. HAL-LE-LU-JAH! HAL-LE-LU-JAH! HAL-
FOR EV-ER AND EV-ER. HAL-LE-LU-JAH! HAL-LE-LU-JAH! HAL-
FOR EV-ER AND EV-ER. HAL-LE-LU-JAH! HAL-LE-LU-JAH! HAL-
PNO.

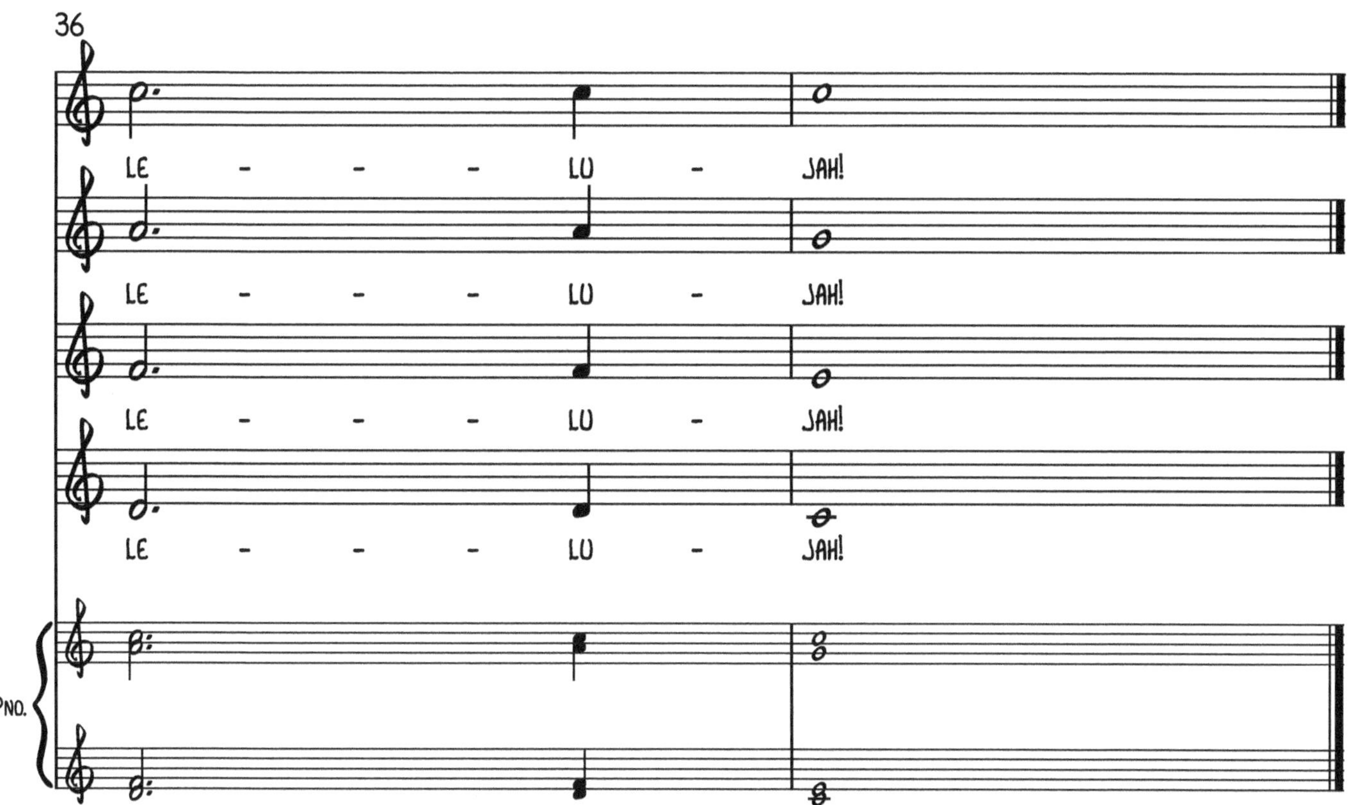
36
LE - - - LU - JAH!
LE - - - LU - JAH!
LE - - - LU - JAH!
LE - - - LU - JAH!
Pno.
HC (SSAA)
11-26-24

HARK! THE HERALD ANGELS SING

HTHAS (SSAA)
12-16-24

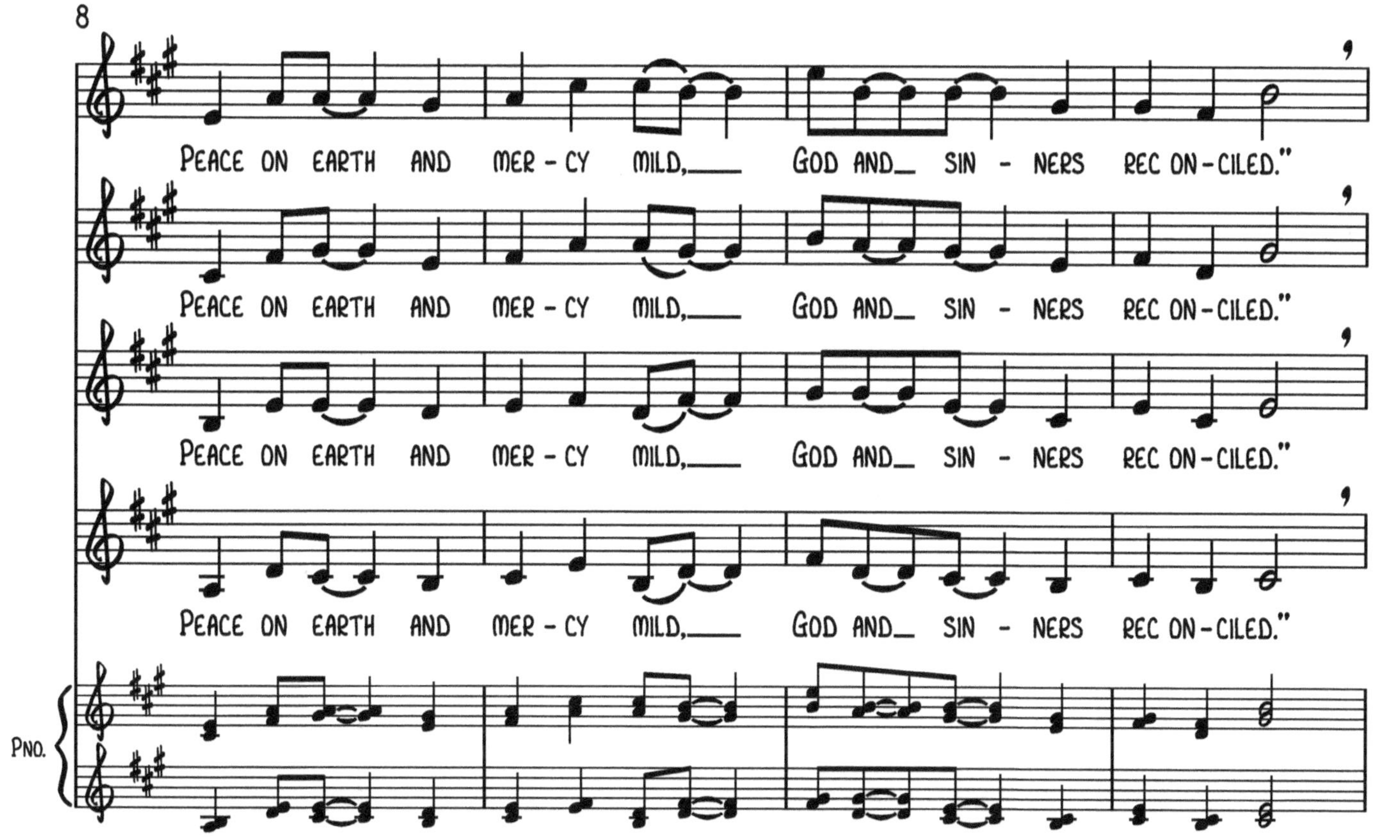

HARK! THE HERALD ANGELS SING
PEACE ON EARTH AND MER-CY MILD, GOD AND SIN-NERS REC ON-CILED."
PEACE ON EARTH AND MER-CY MILD, GOD AND SIN-NERS REC ON-CILED."
PEACE ON EARTH AND MER-CY MILD, GOD AND SIN-NERS REC ON-CILED."
PEACE ON EARTH AND MER-CY MILD, GOD AND SIN-NERS REC ON-CILED."
PNO.
JOY-FUL ALL YE NA-TIONS RISE. JOIN THE TRI-UMPH OF THE SKIES.
JOY-FUL ALL YE NA-TIONS RISE. JOIN THE TRI-UMPH OF THE SKIES.
JOY-FUL ALL YE NA-TIONS RISE. JOIN THE TRI-UMPH OF THE SKIES.
JOY-FUL ALL YE NA-TIONS RISE. JOIN THE TRI-UMPH OF THE SKIES.
JOY-FUL ALL YE NA-TIONS RISE. JOIN THE TRI-UMPH OF THE, SKIES.
PNO.
HTHAS (SSAA)
12-16-24

WITH AN-GEL-IC HOST PRO-CLAIM, "CHRIST IS BORN IN BETH-LE-HEM."
WITH AN-GEL-IC HOST PRO-CLAIM, "CHRIST IS BORN IN BETH-LE-HEM."
WITH AN-GEL-IC HOST PRO-CLAIM, "CHRIST IS BORN IN BETH-LE-HEM."
WITH AN-GEL-IC HOST PRO-CLAIM, "CHRIST IS BORN IN BETH-LE-HEM."
PNO.
HARK! THE HER-ALD AN-GELS SING, "GLO-RY TO THE NEW-BORN KING!" HAIL,
HARK! THE HER-ALD AN-GELS SING, "GLO-RY TO THE NEW-BORN KING!" HAIL,
HARK! THE HER-ALD AN-GELS SING, "GLO-RY TO THE NEW-BORN KING!" HAIL,
HARK! THE HER-ALD AN-GELS SING, "GLO-RY TO THE NEW-BORN KING!" HAIL,
PNO.

HARK! THE HERALD ANGELS SING
24
___ , the heav'n-born Prince of Peace! Hail, the Son_ of Right-eous - ness!
___ , the heav'n-born Prince of Peace! Hail, the Son_ of Right-eous - ness!
___ , the heav'n-born Prince of Peace! Hail, the Son_ of Right-eous - ness!
___ the heav'n-born Prince of Peace!_ Hail, the Son_ of Right-eous - ness!
Pno.
28 
Light and life_ to all He brings,_ ris'n with_ heal - ing in His wings.
Light and life_ to all He brings,_ ris'n with_ heal - ing in His wings.
Light and life_ to all He brings,_ ris'n with_ heal - ing in His wings.
Light and life_ to all He brings,_ ris'n with_ heal - ing in His wings.
Pno.
HTHAS (SSAA)
12-16-24

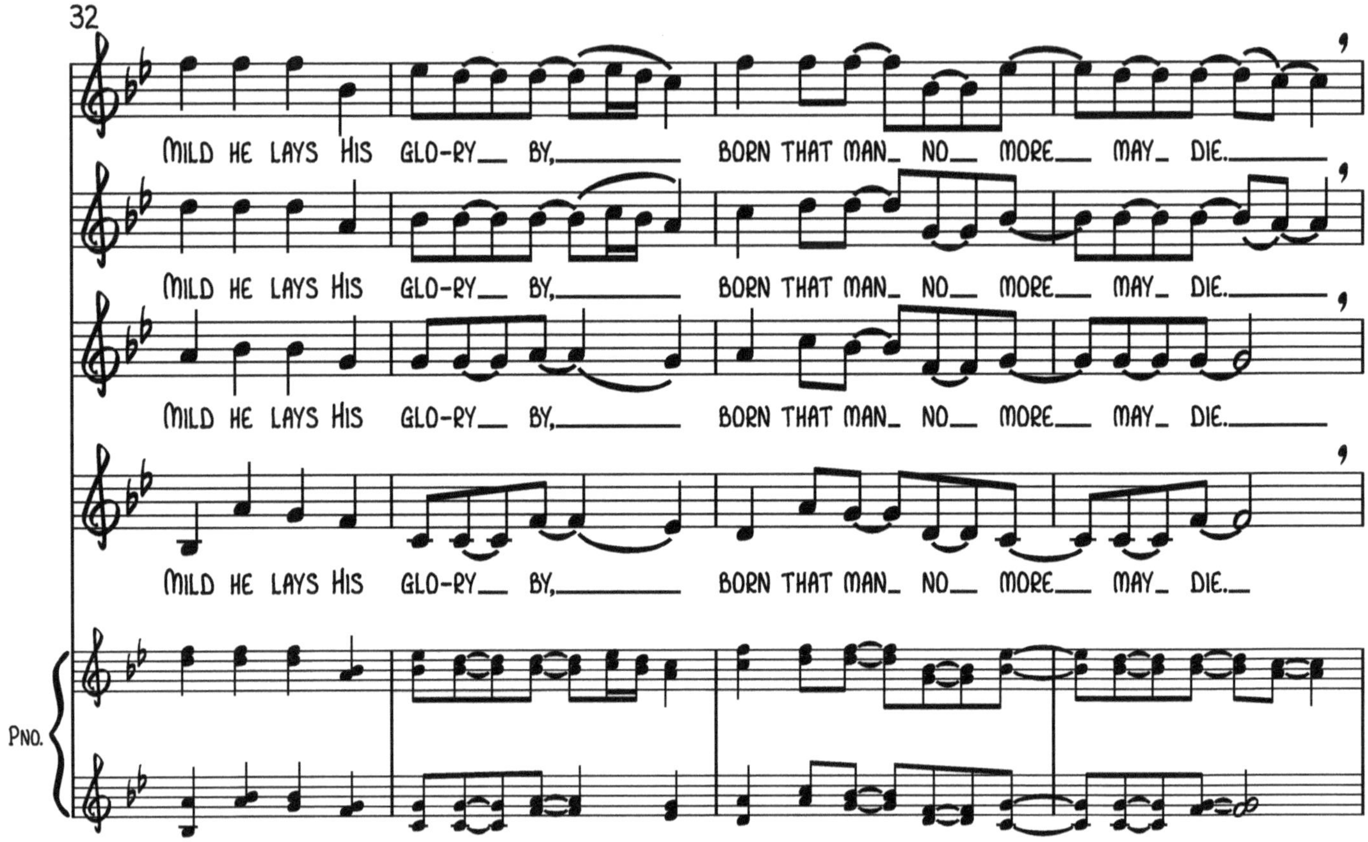

HARK! THE HERALD ANGELS SING

32

MILD HE LAYS HIS GLO-RY__ BY,________ BORN THAT MAN__ NO__ MORE__ MAY__ DIE.________

MILD HE LAYS HIS GLO-RY__ BY,________ BORN THAT MAN__ NO__ MORE__ MAY__ DIE.________

MILD HE LAYS HIS GLO-RY__ BY,________ BORN THAT MAN__ NO__ MORE__ MAY__ DIE.________

MILD HE LAYS HIS GLO-RY__ BY,________ BORN THAT MAN__ NO__ MORE__ MAY__ DIE.__

PNO.

36

BORN TO RAISE THE__ SONG__ OF__ EARTH, BORN TO__ GIVE THEM SEC-OND BIRTH.

BORN TO RAISE THE__ SONG__ OF__ EARTH, BORN TO__ GIVE THEM SEC-OND BIRTH.

BORN TO RAISE THE__ SONG__ OF__ EARTH, BORN TO__ GIVE THEM SEC-OND BIRTH.

BORN TO RAISE THE__ SONG__ OF__ EARTH, BORN TO GIVE THEM SEC-OND BIRTH.

PNO.

HTHAS (SSAA)
12-16-24

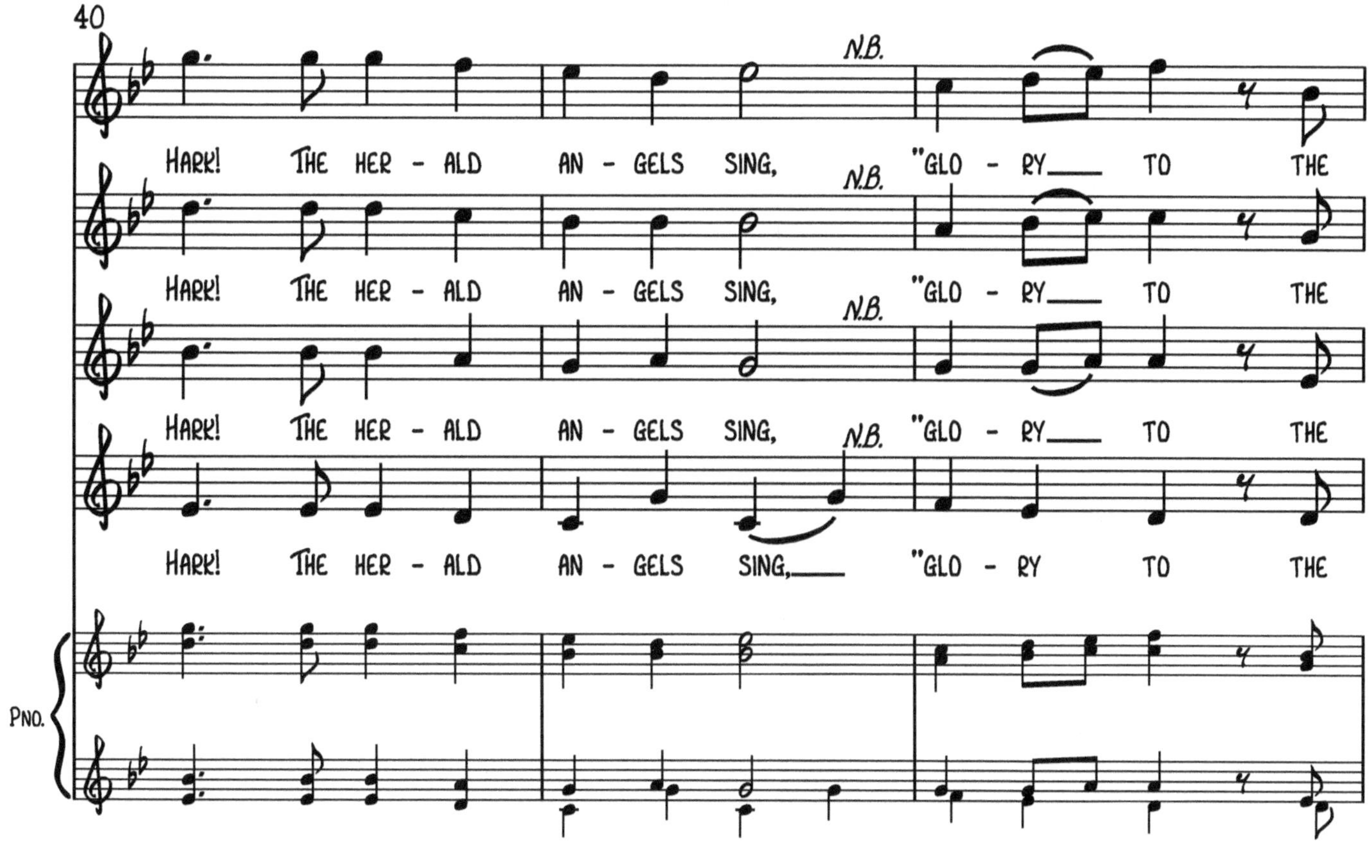

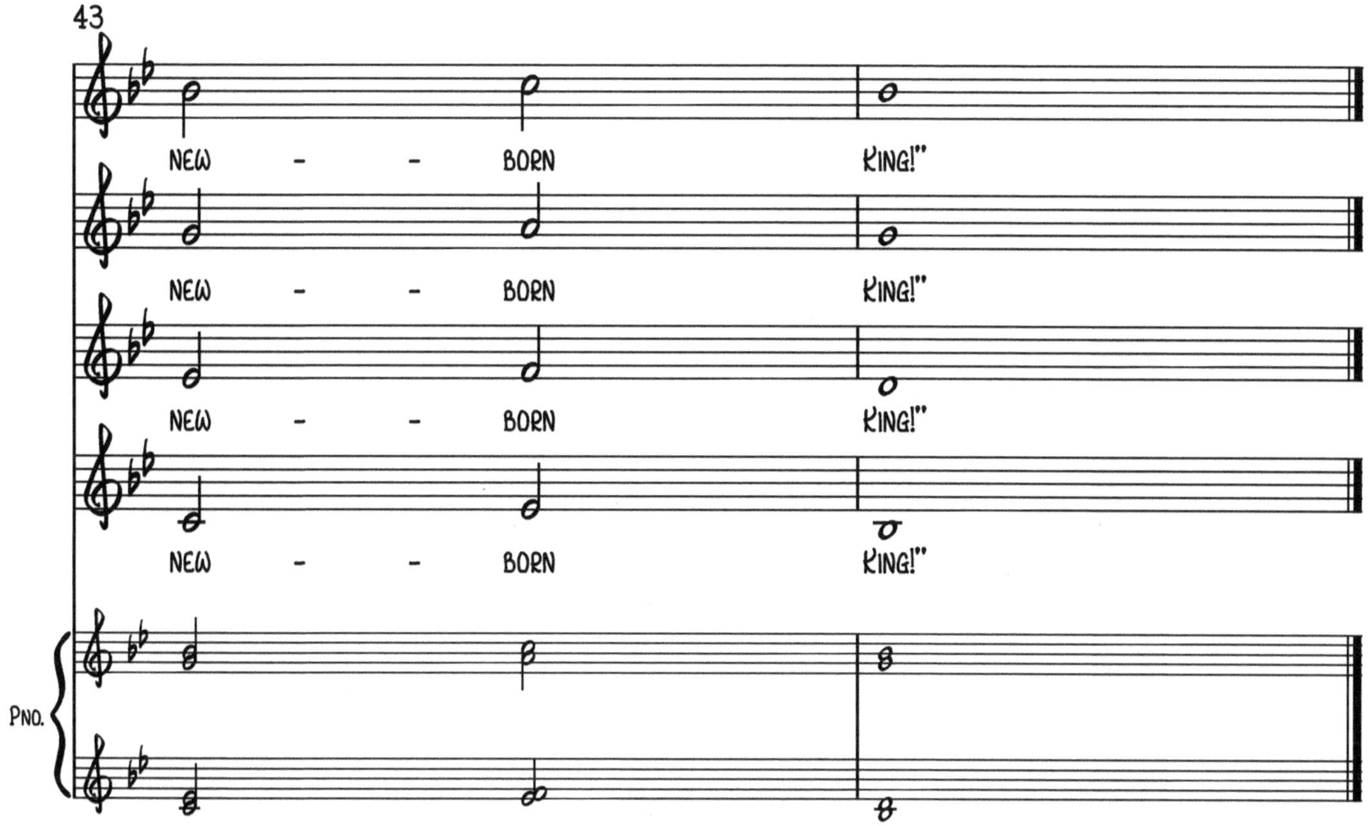

Additional resources for this arrangement

I SAW THREE SHIPS

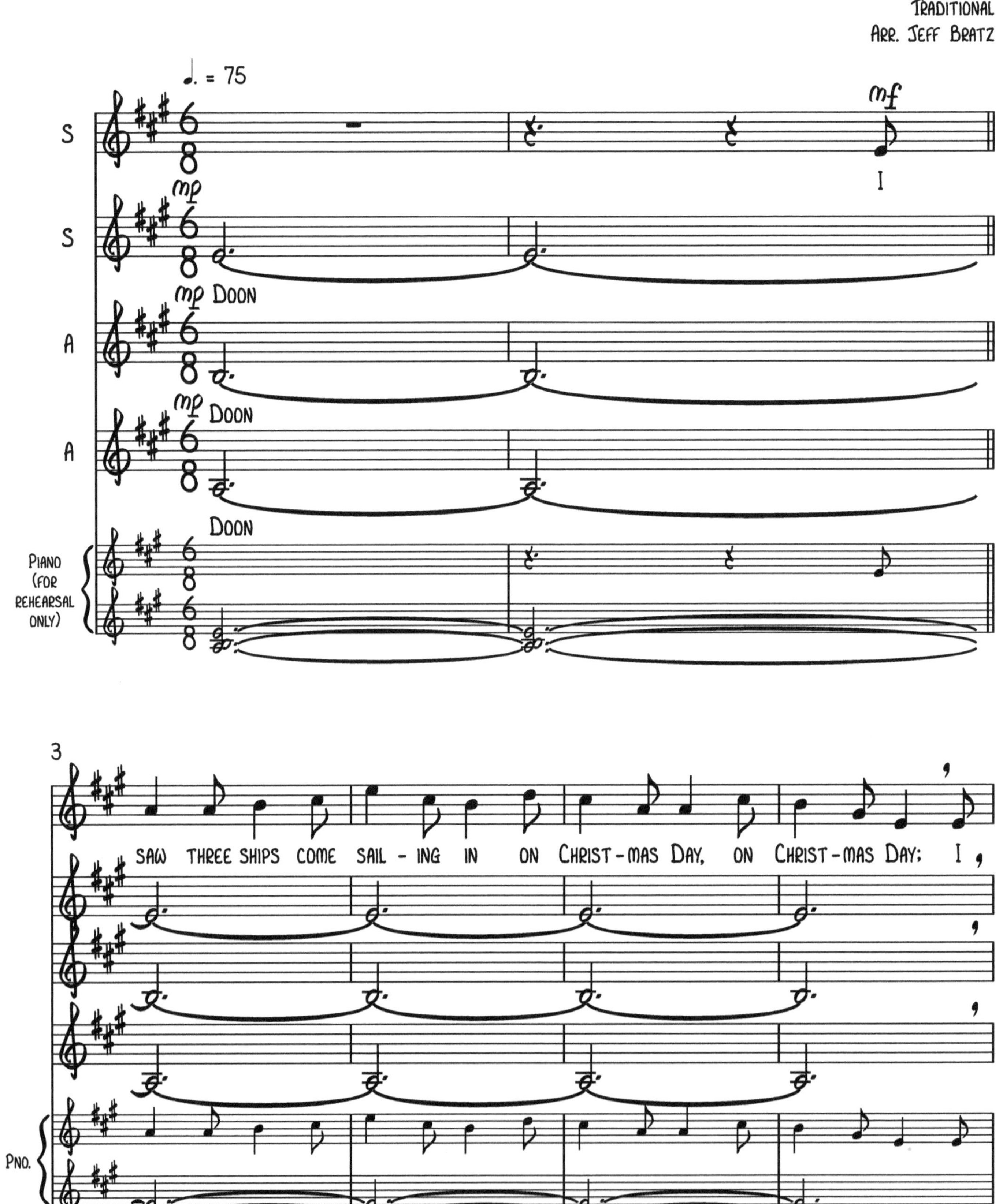

I SAW THREE SHIPS
7
SAW THREE SHIPS COME SAIL - ING IN ON CHRIST - MAS DAY IN THE MORN - ING. PRAY,
mf
DOON
PRAY,
DOON
DOON
PNO.
11
WITH - ER SAILED THOSE SHIPS ALL THREE, ON CHRIST - MAS DAY, ON CHRIST - MAS DAY; PRAY
WITH - ER SAILED THOSE SHIPS ALL THREE, ON CHRIST - MAS DAY, ON CHRIST - MAS DAY; PRAY
DOON
DOON
DOON
DOON
PNO.

ISTS (SSAA)
12-17-24

WITH - ER SAILED THOSE SHIPS ALL THREE, ON CHRIST - MAS DAY IN THE MORN - ING?
WITH - ER SAILED THOSE SHIPS ALL THREE, ON CHRIST - MAS DAY IN THE MORN - ING?
DOON DOON DOON
DOON DOON DOON
THEY SAILED IN - TO BETH - LE - HEM ON CHRIST - MAS DAY, ON CHRIST - MAS DAY;
THEY SAILED IN - TO BETH - LE - HEM ON CHRIST - MAS DAY, ON CHRIST - MAS DAY;
THEY SAILED IN - TO BETH - LE - HEM ON CHRIST - MAS DAY, ON CHRIST - MAS DAY;
THEY SAILED IN - TO BETH - LE - HEM ON CHRIST - MAS DAY, ON CHRIST - MAS DAY;
DOON DOON DOON DOON DOON

23
THEY SAILED IN - TO BETH - LE - HEM ON CHRIST - MAS DAY IN THE MORN - ING. AND
THEY SAILED IN - TO BETH - LE - HEM ON CHRIST - MAS DAY IN THE MORN - ING.
THEY SAILED IN - TO BETH - LE - HEM ON CHRIST - MAS DAY IN THE MORN - ING.
DOON DOON DOON DOON
PNO.
27
mp
mf
ALL THE BELLS ON EARTH SHALL RING ON CHRIST - MAS DAY, ON CHRIST - MAS DAY; AND
mp
AND ALL THE SOULS ON EARTH SHALL SING ON CHRIST - MAS DAY, ON
mp
AND ALL THE BELLS ON EARTH SHALL RING ON
AND ALL THE SOULS ON
PNO.

ALL THE BELLS ON EARTH SHALL RING ON CHRIST-MAS DAY IN THE MORN - ING,
CHRIST-MAS DAY; AND ALL THE SOULS ON EARTH SHALL SING ON CHRIST-MAS DAY IN THE
CHRIST-MAS DAY, ON CHRIST-MAS DAY; AND ALL THE BELLS ON EARTH SHALL RING ON
EARTH SHALL SING ON CHRIST-MAS DAY, ON CHRIST-MAS DAY; AND ALL THE SOULS ON
MORN - ING, MORN - ING, MORN - ING. THEN
MORN - ING, MORN - ING, MORN - ING. THEN
CHRIST - MAS DAY IN THE MORN - ING, MORN - ING, THEN
EARTH SHALL SING ON CHRIST - MAS DAY IN THE MORN - ING, THEN

I SAW THREE SHIPS

ISTS (SSAA)
12-17-24

I SAW THREE SHIPS

THE TWELVE-ISH DAYS OF CHRISTMAS

TTDOC (SSAA)
12-30-24

SE - COND, THIRD, AND FORTH DAYS WERE BIRDS AND BIRDS MORE BIRDS AND THEN A
SE - COND, THIRD, AND FORTH DAYS WERE BIRDS AND BIRDS MORE BIRDS AND THEN A
SE - COND, THIRD, AND FORTH DAYS WERE BIRDS AND BIRDS MORE BIRDS AND THEN A
SE - COND, THIRD, AND FORTH DAYS WERE BIRDS AND BIRDS MORE BIRDS AND THEN A
Pno.
BIRD SIT - TING IN A PEAR TREE.
BIRD SIT - TING IN A PEAR TREE. ON THE
BIRD SIT - TING IN A PEAR TREE. ON THE
BIRD SIT - TING IN A PEAR TREE.
Pno.

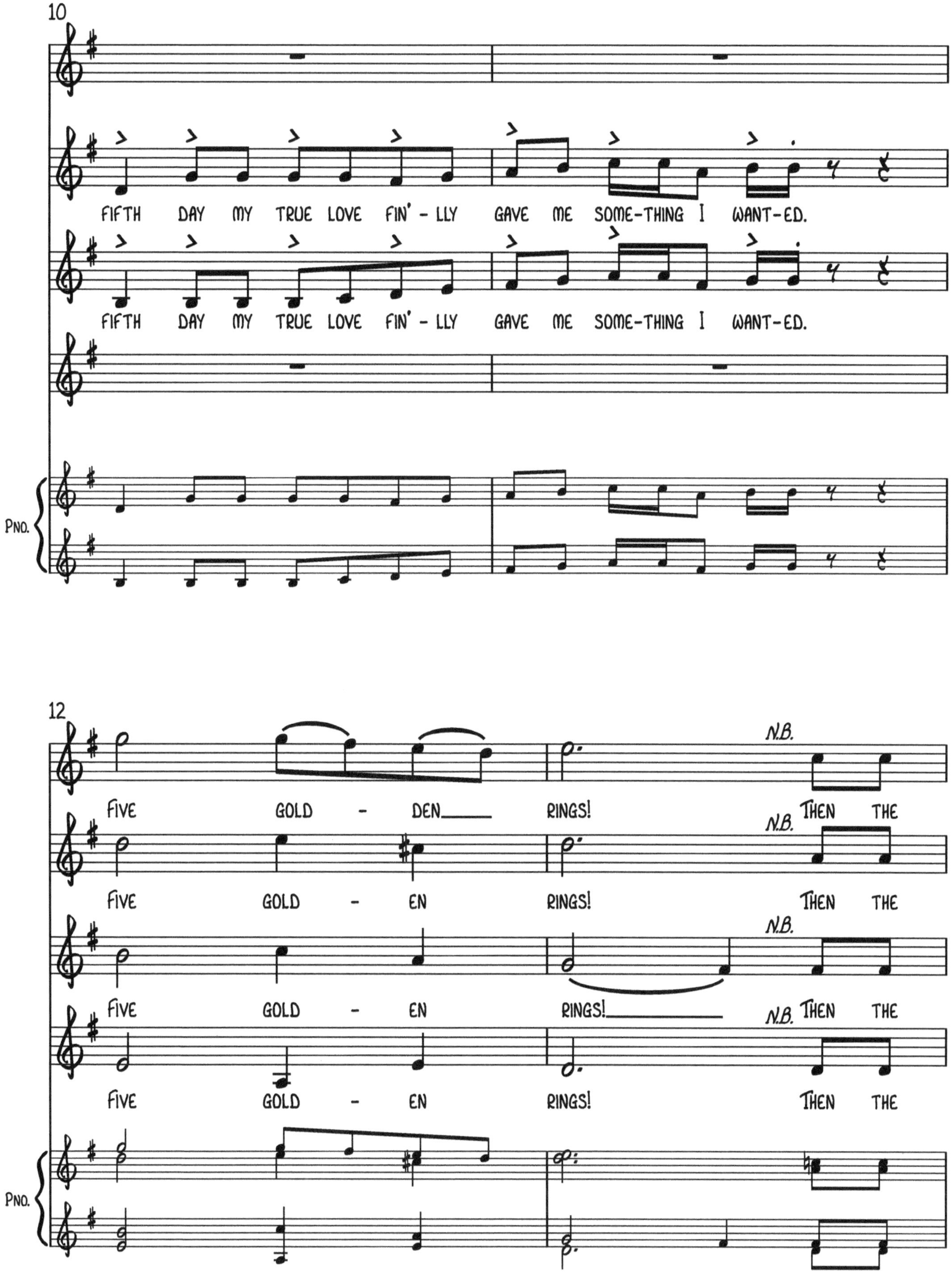
10
FIFTH DAY MY TRUE LOVE FIN' - LLY GAVE ME SOME-THING I WANT-ED.
FIFTH DAY MY TRUE LOVE FIN' - LLY GAVE ME SOME-THING I WANT-ED.
PNO.
12
N.B.
FIVE GOLD - DEN RINGS! THEN THE
N.B.
FIVE GOLD - EN RINGS! THEN THE
N.B.
FIVE GOLD - EN RINGS! THEN THE
N.B.
FIVE GOLD - EN RINGS! THEN THE
PNO.

SUBITO
SIXTH AND SE-VENTH AND EIGHTH AND NINTH AND TENTH AND E - LE-VENTH THEN THE
SIXTH AND SE-VENTH AND EIGHTH AND NINTH AND TENTH AND E - LE-VENTH THEN THE
SIXTH AND SE-VENTH AND EIGHTH AND NINTH AND TENTH AND E - LE-VENTH THEN THE
SIXTH AND SE-VENTH AND EIGHTH AND NINTH AND TENTH AND E - LE-VENTH THEN THE
PNO.
TWELFTH DAY OF CHRIST-MAS MY TRUE LOVE GAVE TO ME
TWELFTH DAY OF CHRIST-MAS MY TRUE LOVE GAVE TO ME
TWELFTH DAY OF CHRIST-MAS MY TRUE LOVE GAVE TO ME
TWELFTH DAY OF CHRIST-MAS MY TRUE LOVE GAVE TO ME
PNO.
1-6
1-6

THE TWELVE-ISH DAYS OF CHRISTMAS

TTDOC (SSAA)
12-30-24

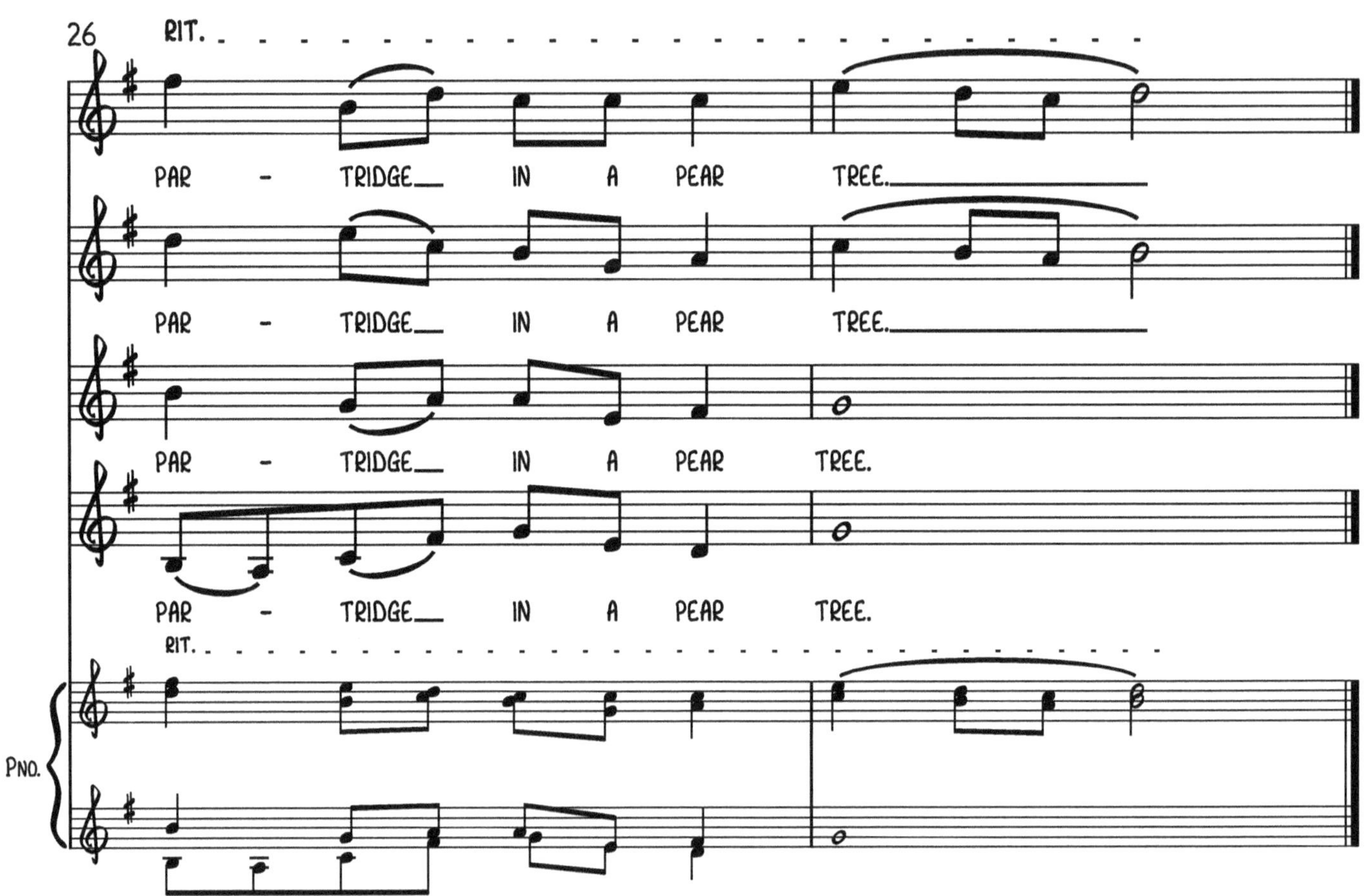
26
RIT.
PAR - TRIDGE IN A PEAR TREE.
PAR - TRIDGE IN A PEAR TREE.
PAR - TRIDGE IN A PEAR TREE.
PAR - TRIDGE IN A PEAR TREE.
RIT.
PNO.

* STAY IN TIME, BUT FEEL FREE TO PLAY WITH THE WORDS *

EX. PEEL OFF EARLY ONE BY ONE TO COMPLAIN ABOUT ALL THE GIFTS, THEN PEEL OFF THE 2ND ALTO AS A VOICE OF REASON. HAVE THE 1ST SOPRANO HAPPILY CONTINUE THE LYRICS ALL THE WAY. BUT ALL SILENT ON BEAT 4 AFTER 'SIX GEESE A-LAYING'.

TWELVE DRUMMERS DRUMMING,
'LEVEN PIPERS PIPING,
TEN LORDS A-LEAPING,
NINE LADIES DANCING,
EIGHT MAIDS A-MILKING,
SEVEN SWANS A-SWIMMING,

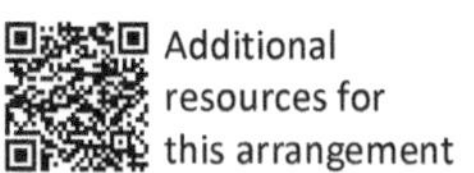
Additional resources for this arrangement

TTDOC (SSAA)
12-30-24

FINAL WORDS

Please consider leaving a review of this book. I would greatly appreciate it. It will help me to continue on this book writing journey I've set off on.

Thank you in advance!

LEAVE A REVIEW

HARMONYTABS EMAIL LIST

Once again, here is the link to the HarmonyTabs email list to keep you up to speed on any new music, publications, and promotions.

ABOUT THE AUTHOR

Jeff Bratz has a degree in Professional Music from the School for Music Vocations and a Professional Certificate in Music Theory and Composition from Berklee College of Music. He's a composer and arranger specializing in vocal arrangements. In a former life, Jeff was a music teacher for grades pre-k through high school. He has sung in dozens of vocal groups including The Dickens Carolers at Disneyland's *Club 33*, The Fault Line on *America's Got Talent*, and Manhattan Transfer tribute group LA Transfer. He was also part of the Downbeat award-winning First Take. He currently performs with rock band RaDIUM, 80s rock tribute band 8IGHTY 6IXX, and salsa band Calle Mambo. He lives in Massachusetts with his wonderful partner Kristen and the cutest nugget that ever nuggeted: Ollie!